Culture + Leisure Services
Red Doles Lane
Hudders

D0490445

START AND RUN YOUR
OWN BUSINESS

If you want to know how ...

Watching the Bottom Line

Financial Management for Small Businesses

The Ultimate Business Plan

Essential planning skills to get you where you want to be

Setting Up and Running a Complementary Health Practice

The insider guide to making a living from running a complementary health practice

100 Ways to Make Your Business a Success

A resource book for small businesses

How To Books
Spring Hill House
Spring Hill Road
Begbroke, Oxford
OX5 IRX
United Kingdom
E-mail: info@howtobooks.co.uk
http://www.howtobooks.co.uk

START AND RUN YOUR OWN BUSINESS

The complete guide to setting up and
managing a small business

Second edition

Alan Le Marinel

Published by How To Books Ltd,
Spring Hill House, Spring Hill Road,
Begbroke, Oxford OX5 1RX. United Kingdom.
Tel: (01865) 375794. Fax: (01865) 379162
email: info@howtobooks.co.uk
http://www.howtobooks.co.uk

First edition 2001
Second edition 2005
Reprinted 2005
Reprinted 2006

British Library Cataloguing in Publication Data.
A catalogue record for this book is available from the British Library.

ISBN 10: 1-85703-988-2
ISBN 13: 978-1-85703-988-7

Edited by Francesca Mitchell
Cover design by Baseline Arts Ltd, Oxford
Produced for How To Books by Deer Park Productions, Tavistock
Typeset by Pantek Arts Ltd, Maidstone, Kent
Printed and bound in Great Britain by Bell & Bain Ltd., Glasgow

NOTE: The material contained in this book is set out in good faith for general guidance and no liability can
be accepted for loss or expense incurred as a result of relying in particular circumstances on statements
made in this book. Laws and regulations are complex and liable to change, and readers should check the
current position with the relevant authorities before making personal arrangements.

Contents

Preface

Running your own business can be a very rewarding and fulfilling experience. On the other hand it can be difficult, time-consuming, costly, and both physically and mentally draining. You also need to remember the very real statistic that only one in five of all new businesses will survive the first five years of trading.

It is absolutely essential that you have the right reasons for wanting to start and run your own business. If the idea of establishing a business is the only option that you have then I would strongly urge you to think again. It is not an easy option and unless you consider that it is the right option for you, it is more than likely you will become one of the failure statistics.

However, if you have decided that you really want to start your own business then this is the book for you. It covers all the essential points you need to know and think about before you actually go ahead. Even if you already operate your own business, it will prove invaluable in contributing to your ongoing success.

There are no secret tricks to being successful in business. Success will only come through hard work and through always offering something that the consumer wants, at the right price, in the right place, and in the right quantity. On a final note, you must always remember that you must never lose sight of the fact that you are also in business to make money. Without ongoing profits you will eventually fail.

Alan Le Marinel

1

Thinking through your idea

Before you can consider starting your business you need to be sure that you actually have the right reasons for wanting to run a business in the first place. Wanting to run your own business because you have no other option is definitely not the right reason. It is important to see the creation of your own business as an opportunity to do something that you really want to do. Some typical reasons could include:

◆ to make money
◆ to gain independence
◆ to be involved in something that interests you.

There is nothing wrong with the first two, but the third reason is one of the most common. Many small businesses evolve from hobbies or part-time activities that actually expand into money-making opportunities. This is fine provided the business can generate sufficient profit to earn you a good living.

This is one aspect that you need to be absolutely clear about from the outset. Your business must generate enough profit to reward you for the time and money that you will invest. Unless it does this you would be better shelving your ideas for a business and investing your money in a building society savings account.

TIP
Write down and consider carefully your reasons for starting a business – are they realistic rather than idealistic?

GAINING THE SUPPORT OF YOUR FAMILY

Running your own business can have a dramatic effect on your family life so it is vital that you have their support before you start. If you have previously been in employment you can say goodbye to the standard nine to five working life. You may also find that your home life and your business life suddenly become intertwined.

If you are giving up a job to start your own business, the regular salary or wage payments will also cease. Your income will depend entirely on how successful your business becomes.

Working for yourself is not an easy option. It will require hard work with the probability of long hours. Paid holidays and days off sick will be a thing of the past. Weekends will also probably be encroached upon to enable you to deal with basic administration.

Unless you have support from your family, you will be fighting to survive on two separate fronts – at home and at work. You cannot afford these distractions. You must be able to concentrate your efforts on running your business.

DO YOU HAVE THE SKILLS REQUIRED TO RUN A BUSINESS?

At this stage it might help if you consider your answers to the following questions:

- ◆ Are you hard-working and self-disciplined?
- ◆ How enthusiastic and motivated are you?
- ◆ Can you work under severe pressure?
- ◆ Do you take logical, structured decisions?
- ◆ How well do you get on with people?

◆ Are you willing to take advice?

◆ How is your health and general well-being?

It doesn't matter if you cannot give positive answers to all of the above. You'll at least discover which you most need help with.

If you are leaving a job to start your own business there is a further test you can apply in order to ascertain whether you have what it takes to run a successful business. You may be very good at doing the work that your boss asks you to do but look at the position from the other side, could you do the work that your boss does? That is what running a business is all about – no longer working for someone but actually setting yourself tasks to do.

WHAT SORT OF BUSINESS DO YOU WANT TO START?

You don't need a new innovative idea with which to start a business. There are, in fact, very few business start-ups that offer something that isn't already available. The key point is that if you are going to offer something that can be bought elsewhere, you need to persuade your customers that they should buy from *you* rather than your competitor.

This is one of the most crucial, and often the most misunderstood aspects of running a business. Always have some form of competitive advantage. This could include:

◆ lower prices

◆ longer opening hours

◆ better quality of service

◆ offer of extended guarantees or maintenance periods

◆ faster speed of response in the event of breakdown.

TIP

Write down all the types of business you think you can start with the expertise that you have – refine these down to give you two or three options.

Of course, the actual advantages that you could offer will depend upon your business.

HOW WILL I START MY BUSINESS?

There are three ways in which you can start your own business:

- ◆ start your business from scratch
- ◆ buy a franchised business
- ◆ buy an existing business.

Starting from scratch

Starting your own business from scratch is undoubtedly the riskiest way of starting a business. However, it can also be the most satisfying.

There is no mythical or secret formula to establishing a business that is guaranteed to succeed. You only need to compare the Stock Exchange list of the top 100 companies from 10 years ago to those of today to see that even the largest companies can fail.

To stand the greatest chance of survival it is essential that you undertake substantial research into the market and, more importantly, research the market on an ongoing basis to stay ahead of the competition. You must also start small. Many small business start-ups suffer from delusions of grandeur and spend money on totally unnecessary items.

TIP

Time spent researching the market now will pay dividends later – don't be in a rush to start your business with only a small amount of information.

When you start your business you need to adopt a minimal approach. If you spend money on unnecessary items, to make your business 'look good' then you are only fooling yourself.

You are also increasing your expenditure, thereby lowering your profits. In starting your business you will need as much profit as you can obtain, not only to pay your own salary but also to provide funds in reserve for expansion. Think small to start with and you stand a chance of growing. Think big to start with and you will probably fail.

Whilst the majority of this book concentrates on starting your business from scratch, at this stage there is one further small piece of advice you should consider. Only start your own business in an area in which you have some expertise or knowledge. Remember, whatever sort of business you establish you are going to come up against competition. Unless your business expertise and knowledge is at least on a par with those competitors you will be starting at a disadvantage.

Buying a franchised business

As an alternative to starting your own business from scratch consider buying a franchise. A franchise is a business that has already been tested in the market and proven to be a success. Remember, however, that it is the concept itself that has been proven and that alone will not guarantee success for you.

Franchising is really an informal partnership. The franchisor will want to ensure that your business is launched successfully and that it remains profitable. Their income as well as yours will depend on your success. This creates a bond between the two parties in terms of a close dependence on each other. Buying a franchise will allow you to run your own business, but unlike a new start-up business you will have the ongoing help and assistance from the franchisor to make it a success. As with all businesses, there will be risks, but a franchise should reduce those risks. Statistically the number of business failures relating to franchises is far less than those relating to new start-up businesses.

Franchising is not an easy option. It can, however, make running your own business a lot easier. Franchising is looked at in greater depth in Chapter 18.

Buying an existing business

You may consider that buying an established business might be the easiest and safest way of running your own business. This may not necessarily be the case. There are all sorts of pitfalls that you could encounter. The first will probably be actually reaching agreement on what the value of the business is and how much the purchase price should be.

You may also need to investigate thoroughly the reasons for the business being put up for sale. If it is making money and is profitable why should the existing owner wish to sell? Even if the reason is a good one, for example, the retirement of the existing owner, you will often find that their value of the business is overstated on a true commercial basis.

Some businesses are also built around the reputation of the owner so you will need to consider what will happen when they leave. Will the existing customer base transfer their loyalty to you as the new owner or will they now go elsewhere?

Buying an existing business is fraught with danger so professional help is an absolute necessity before you make any commitment. Chapter 19 looks at the question of buying an existing business in more detail.

INVESTING IN YOUR OWN BUSINESS

In order to start your own business you are going to have to make an investment in that business. This investment can take two main forms:
◆ financial
◆ non-financial.

Financial investment, as the name suggests, is a direct injection of cash into your business. If you are operating as a limited liability company, this could take the form of share capital or director's loan. If you operate either as a sole trader or partnership, it will be classified as owner's or partner's capital.

The decision as to which type of business to operate can be complex. There are advantages and disadvantages to operating as a sole trader or as a partnership or as a limited liability company. All of these alternatives are explained in the next chapter.

Non-financial investment is the introduction of assets that you may already own. For example, motor vehicles and tools and equipment. These need to be carefully valued for inclusion in your financial records. If you are introducing assets into your business in this way you are advised to seek the help of an accountant. This will ensure that your assets are correctly valued and that they comply with any Inland Revenue guidelines.

Showing commitment

There are no hard and fast rules about how much of your own money you must invest in your business. However, if you are looking to raise external finance then any potential funder will need to be satisfied that your contribution is sufficient. One of the important factors that the potential lender will be looking for is that you are showing a total commitment to your business. Basically, if you are not personally prepared to risk sufficient funds, the lender is unlikely to either.

> **TIP**
>
> You will need at least some element of cash to invest in your business – have a look at the assets that you own and see if some can be sold to raise money.

2
Complying with Legislation

Legislation affecting businesses has increased greatly over the past few years and it is absolutely essential that you understand any laws that could impact upon your business. It is also essential, if any law does affect your business, that you comply with it in full. Remember, ignorance of the law is no excuse.

It would be impossible to give even a brief outline of the legislation that could impact upon all businesses. This is where you will need specific advice for the type of business that you are establishing. Chapter 5 will give you details of some of the business support organisations that can help you in this respect.

In this chapter we will look at some of the legislation that will affect all businesses. This will include the different forms of business that you can start, together with the basic requirements of the Inland Revenue for tax and National Insurance, and HM Customs and Excise for VAT registration and payment. We will also look at how you can protect your business using the legislation covering patents, trademarks and copyright.

A WORD OF WARNING TO START THIS CHAPTER
In recent years there have been a number of scams regarding legislation issues operated on the unwary new business. In some cases experienced entrepreneurs have even been caught out by the unscrupulous.

At the time of writing there are at least two scams being operated regarding:

- fake Health and Safety registration agencies
- fake Data Protection Act registration agencies.

Fake Health and Safety registration agencies

The Office of Fair Trading have issued warnings against a number of fake agencies and advised that any demand for payment should be ignored and reported in order that they can take appropriate action. These agencies include:

- Health and Safety Enforcement Agency (HSEA)
- Health and Safety Compliance Agency (HSCA)
- Health and Safety Registration Enforcement Division (HSRED)

The advice from the 'real' Health and Safety Executive (HSE) is that they never write to firms seeking advance payment for any services which it has not provided. If you receive any correspondence regarding health and safety matters then contact your local HSE office before making any payment.

Fake Data Protection Act registration agencies

Businesses are receiving letters and demands for payment from unofficial companies offering Data Protection registration services.

The advice from the Data Protection Comissioner's office is that if you are unsure whether you need to register, or you need information or help with registration, then you should contact them. There is absolutely no need to use the services of an agency.

There are bound to be variations on these scams and if you are in any doubt as to their authenticity you are strongly advised to make enquiries with a business support organisation, for example Business Link, before you part with any money.

THE DIFFERENT FORMS OF BUSINESS

There are a number of different forms that a business can take and there is no prescriptive method by which you can decide which one is right for you. Whilst there are other options, most new businesses start in one of three forms:

◆ sole trader
◆ partnership
◆ limited company.

Sole trader

This is the simplest way of starting a business with very few formalities. You will need to advise the Inland Revenue that you are self-employed for tax and National Insurance contributions. They will provide the relevant guidance booklet and notification form upon request.

Control of the business will be entirely yours and you will be responsible for all management decisions. You will, however, also be personally responsible for any debts that you incur and, should your business fail, any personal assets that you have can be seized and sold to repay those debts.

On the plus side, any profits that you make will belong to you. Moreover, whilst you have a responsibility to maintain proper accounting records for tax and VAT purposes, any records that you keep are not available for public inspection.

Partnerships

If you are going to start your business with one or more other people you could form a partnership. In effect, this is the same as a sole trader with all the partners sharing responsibility for managing the business. The same applies to any debts of the partnership, in that each partner is personally liable.

In some cases, it may be necessary for a 'Deed of Partnership' to be drawn up. Whilst this is not required by law it can be useful to resolve disputes or where, for example, the profits of the business are not to be shared equally. You may also consider the option of establishing your business as a limited partnership. Whilst the basic concept of limited partnerships has been available for some time, new legislation has been introduced to widen the scope of such partnerships. You will need to seek specialist advice from a solicitor. You can also obtain guidance notes from Companies House free of charge.

> **TIP**
>
> If you are starting a business as a partnership make sure you will be able to work with the potential partner – a partnership can easily fail when the partners fall out.

Company

There are four main types of company:

- **Private company limited by shares** – members' liability is limited to the amount unpaid on shares they hold.
- **Private company limited by guarantee** – members' liability is limited to the amount they have agreed to contribute to the company's assets if it is wound up.

- ◆ **Private unlimited company** – there is no limit to the members' liability.
- ◆ **Public limited company (PLC)** – the company's shares may be offered for sale to the general public and members' liability is limited to the amount unpaid on shares held by them.

By far the most common limited company established by new businesses is the first example, a private company limited by shares. Whilst you can form a limited company yourself, the easiest way is to purchase one 'off the shelf'. Ready-made companies are available from company formation agents whose names and addresses appear in the *Yellow Pages*. There are also numerous advertisements in the business section of the quality daily newspapers.

In return for a modest fee, usually between £50 and £100, you can purchase a company that has already been registered at Companies House and is ready to start trading. Most of these 'off the shelf' companies will have obscure names, for example Delta 5671 Ltd, which have been used merely to gain registration. Subject to acceptance by Companies House you can, however, easily change the name of your company to something more meaningful to your business.

The legislation relating to the operation of a limited company is extremely complex so seek the help of a qualified accountant. You can also obtain free guidance notes from Companies House either through their website or by telephoning 029 2038 0801.

> **TIP**
> Your accountant should ensure that the appropriate returns are filed correctly, although ultimately it is the responsibility of the directors of the company to ensure that this is done.

There are strict requirements concerning the accounting records that a limited company must maintain. Copies of accounts are subject to public inspection and must therefore be filed with Companies House. The amount of information that needs to be disclosed will depend on the size of your company. There are some exemptions available to smaller companies.

DECIDING ON A BUSINESS NAME

Once you have chosen which form your business will take the next step is to decide on an appropriate business name. You may decide to use your own name as your business name. If, however, you are going to trade under another name, you will need to comply with the requirements of the Business Names Act 1985.

This Act affects all forms of businesses, whether sole trader, partnerships or companies. It applies to:

◆ A company which trades under a name which is not its corporate name, 'AB Limited' trading as 'AB Engineering', for example.
◆ A partnership which does not trade under the names of all the partners.
◆ An individual who trades under a name which is not his or her surname.

Whilst you can use virtually any name that you please there are some words that you cannot use without specific permission from the Secretary of State for Trade and Industry. These include words which imply national or international pre-eminence, for example:

◆ British
◆ International
◆ United Kingdom
◆ European
◆ National.

In the same way, you cannot use words which imply business preeminence or representative status without specific permission. Examples include:

◆ Association
◆ Council
◆ Institution
◆ Authority
◆ Federation
◆ Society
◆ Board
◆ Institute.

Under the Act there are also strict requirements as to disclosure of the owners of a business which is using a trading name. You will need to disclose:

◆ the corporate name; or
◆ the name of each partner; or
◆ the individual person's name; and
◆ in relation to each person named, an address at which documents can be served.

You will need to show this information clearly in all:

◆ the places where you carry on your business and where you deal with customers or suppliers
◆ business letters
◆ written orders for the supply of goods or services
◆ invoices and receipts
◆ written demands for the payment of business debts.

Failure to comply with any of the requirements of the Act is a criminal offence and you therefore need to establish your obligations at an early stage. You can seek guidance from Companies House which provides a free booklet explaining the exact implications of the Business Names Act 1985.

Checking whether your business name is already being used

There is no longer any legal requirement for you to register a trading name. If, however, you copy another business's name or trademark, whether innocently or not, it could lead to legal action being taken against you. Potentially this could result in the closure of your business. Even though a limited company will have its name checked to ensure that there is no identical company already in existence, Companies House does not check for similar names as sole traders or partnerships or for any registered trademarks and so the risk is the same.

The easiest way to protect yourself in this respect is to use the services of Business Names Registrations plc (BNR), which has access to databases covering over 2,000,000 business names, 1,000,000 limited companies and 600,000 registered trademarks, all updated monthly.

For a small fee, BNR will check your business name and add it to their register, which will help protect you against anyone else using the same name. You will also receive information on matters affecting business names and ownership through a regular BNR newsletter.

PROTECTING YOUR BUSINESS IDEAS

Copyright and patent laws are available to protect your ideas being exploited by another person. They can also prevent someone using your 'intellectual property' without your permission. Your business name and logo can be protected by registering them as a trademark.

TIP

Your business name and trademark could become extremely valuable assets of your business – make sure you protect them.

Patents

If you have invented something unique, consider applying for a patent to stop anyone else producing anything similar. Applying for a patent is an extremely complicated process and you will need professional help from a patent agent. Most important is that you must not discuss or disclose your idea to anyone else before you apply for a patent. Once the idea is in 'the public domain' it is unlikely that you will gain any protection.

Copyright

Copyright is the creator's legal rights over works such as:

◆ paintings
◆ photographs
◆ writings.

Unlike patents, which need to be registered, copyright happens automatically. This means that as I sit here writing this book I am automatically creating a copyright. Unless I assign that copyright to someone else it remains with me. At the front of this book you will see '© Alan Le Marinel' which is the publisher's acknowledgement of my copyright.

Trademarks

Once you have chosen a name for your business, your products or your business logo, you can protect all of them by applying for a trademark to be registered. You can gain free information on registering a trademark from the Trademarks Registry at the Patent Office.

KEEPING THE INLAND REVENUE HAPPY

If you start your own business as a sole trader or partnership you will come under the Inland Revenue Self Assessment scheme for the payment of income tax and National Insurance contributions (NI). A limited company will also be liable for Corporation Tax. As an employee of that company you will pay income tax and National Insurance contributions in the same way as any other employee.

National Insurance contributions

There are three classes of NI contributions:

- ◆ **Class One** – applies to all employed people and is paid by both the employer and the employee.
- ◆ **Class Two** – paid at a flat rate by all self-employed people whether they are sole traders or partners.
- ◆ **Class Three** – payable by the self-employed as a percentage of profits between a minimum and maximum level.

As a sole trader you will initially need to pay Class Two contributions. The amount of Class Three contributions will be assessed when you complete your Self Assessment Tax Return.

Dealing with your Self Assessment Tax Return

The best way to deal with your Self Assessment Tax Return is to use an accountant to prepare the figures and complete the return for you. Their services will incur a fee but any amount payable (and unless your tax affairs are extremely complicated such an amount should not exceed a few hundred pounds) should be recoverable through the tax savings they can make for you.

TIP

Tax evasion is illegal, but tax avoidance, i.e. making the most of all the allowances available to you, is perfectly acceptable.

Remember that even if you do delegate the completion of your tax return to your accountant *you* are still responsible for ensuring that the return is lodged on time. There are strict penalties for not filing your tax return on time. You could also be liable for interest on any tax that is overdue for payment.

REGISTERING FOR VALUE ADDED TAX (VAT)

Whatever form of business you have chosen, you are going to have to consider the implications of VAT on your business. VAT is a tax that businesses charge when they supply their goods and services within the UK. It is also charged on goods and some services that are imported from outside the European Union (EU) and on goods coming into the UK from another EU member state.

VAT rates

At present there are three VAT rates:

TIP

Examples of zero-rated supplies include most food, books, newspapers, and young children's clothing.

◆ 17.5% – standard rate charged on most goods and services
◆ 5% – reduced rate charged on domestic fuel and power and by charities
◆ 0% – zero rate where no VAT is charged.

How does VAT work?

If the turnover of your business exceeds a certain limit, usually defined in the government's annual budget, you become a 'taxable person' and as such you must register for VAT. Following registration you then account to HM Customs and Excise for VAT whenever you supply goods or services.

The supplies are your 'outputs' and the tax you charge is your 'output tax'. If your customers are also registered for VAT, and the supplies are for their own business, your supplies to them are their 'inputs' and the tax you charge them is their 'input tax'. VAT that you are charged becomes your 'input tax'.

When you account to HM Customs and Excise it is done on a net basis. In other words, you take your 'input tax' from your 'output tax' and only remit the difference. If your 'input tax' is greater than your 'output tax' you can claim the difference back from HM Customs and Excise.

Voluntary registration for VAT

Even if your taxable turnover is below the threshold you can still apply for voluntary registration. There are advantages and disadvantages to voluntary registration and you will need the advice of your accountant before you make any application.

One of the main advantages of voluntary registration for businesses that supply zero-rated goods, is that they can claim back all of their 'input tax'. The major disadvantage, however, is the additional work that will be involved in actually completing the VAT returns.

> **TIP**
>
> Once you are registered for VAT your accounting records must be available for inspection by HM Customs and Excise at any time.

Completing VAT returns and making payment of the tax

VAT returns are usually required every three months and you can apply to have the cycle coincide with your business year-end. Your return, and any tax payable, must be delivered to HM Customs and Excise within one month after the end of the return date. Even if no tax is payable you must still file the return.

In certain circumstances you can apply for alternatives to the normal three-month return requirement.

Monthly VAT returns

You can request monthly returns if you normally expect to receive a refund of VAT rather than having to make payment. If, however, you have registered voluntarily, monthly returns are not an option.

Non-standard VAT returns

If your accounting system is not based on calendar months you can apply for VAT return dates that fit more closely with your system. If you are granted approval in this respect you will be issued with a special certificate detailing the dates on which your VAT returns are to be made.

Annual returns

If you have been registered for VAT for at least 12 months and your business has a taxable turnover below a set threshold, you can apply to make annual VAT returns. Under this scheme you account for VAT by making nine monthly payments based on an estimate of the annual VAT that will be due from you. You then send in your annual return with a final balance payment two months after the end of the year. In some instances, where the likely amount of VAT due is relatively small, there are variations to the annual VAT return scheme that do not require monthly instalments.

Cash accounting scheme

This is another scheme available to businesses with taxable turnover below a defined level. It allows you to account for VAT on the basis of payments received and made rather than on the invoices you issue and receive. This can be particularly beneficial if you allow your customers lengthy periods of trade credit or you have a high incidence of bad debts.

Further details regarding the implications of VAT and guidance notes for businesses can be obtained free of charge from the HM Customs and Excise National Advice Service.

TRADING LAWS THAT MIGHT AFFECT YOUR BUSINESS

At the start of this chapter, I mentioned that it would be impossible to outline all the legislation that could affect your business. The following Acts of Parliament are, however, important to all businesses:

- ◆ Consumer Protection Act 1987
- ◆ Trade Descriptions Acts 1968 and 1972
- ◆ Sale of Goods Act 1979
- ◆ Health and Safety at Work Act 1974.

You will need to seek specialist advice on the exact implications of each of the above on your business but, as far as your customers are concerned, there are three trading standards that will affect you:

- ◆ Any goods that you sell must be **fit for their purpose**. If goods are faulty, your customers have the right to a full refund. Alternatively, you can agree to repair or replace the faulty goods.
- ◆ The goods that you sell must **live up to any claims** that you make about them. It is a criminal offence to make a false claim about your goods or to label goods incorrectly.
- ◆ Goods must meet certain **safety standards**. If a product that you sell is faulty and causes injury, a claim for damages could be made against you.

TIP

Discuss your plans for a business with appropriate advisors who can outline the legislation that is going to have a direct impact on your business.

Businesses that require special licences to trade

There are a number of businesses that require a special licence before they can start to trade. Examples include:

◆ betting shops
◆ cafés and restaurants
◆ children's nurseries
◆ employment agencies
◆ food manufacturers
◆ pet shops
◆ sales of alcohol or tobacco.

This is not an exhaustive list. The important point is that if your business does require a licence you must obtain that licence before you start trading. The penalties for trading without a licence can be severe and your business will be closed down by the relevant authority.

3
Setting Objectives

Before starting your business, consider carefully what your business objectives will be. Business objectives relate to your business as a whole and are your vision of what your business will achieve. These objectives should also be both long and short-term.

Short-term objectives will relate to what you want to achieve in the next 12 months, long-term objectives to what you will want your business to achieve over say, the next five years. You should not confuse business objectives with marketing objectives. Your business objectives are the primary objectives of your business, marketing objectives entirely secondary. Until you have set the overall strategy for your business with appropriate business objectives you cannot consider your marketing objectives.

When you consider any objectives for your business you should ensure that they meet the 'SMART' criteria.

SETTING SMART OBJECTIVES

All of the objectives that you set for your business must be:

- ◆ Specific
- ◆ Measurable
- ◆ Agreed
- ◆ Realistic
- ◆ Timed.

> **TIP**
>
> A crucial step in using the SMART criteria is being aware of how you aim to achieve the objective. There is little point in having an objective if you do not have an appropriate strategy in place to achieve it.

For a new business, your business objectives will probably be few in number. In your first year of trading your only objective may be to make sufficient profit to enable you to achieve a decent standard of living. As the business grows, the number of objectives will probably increase. These could cover such areas as:

◆ achieving increased profitability
◆ reducing overhead expenses in relation to sales
◆ achieving greater production efficiency
◆ making greater use of technology to improve communication.

All of the above are singular in nature, i.e. they are objectives that have only one component. You may also set objectives that link various parts of your business. For example, consider the following hypothetical objective for a distribution business:

To improve the quality of customer service over the next 12 months by reducing delivery times to an average of three days after taking the initial order from the customer.

Having set the objective you'll then need to state exactly how you aim to achieve it. Effectively, you link the objective to a strategy. Continuing with the same hypothetical example this might read:

We will achieve this improvement by the introduction of a new distribution system which will take advantage of the latest computer technology to track the order, stock and delivery systems.

As you can see, this objective meets all of the SMART criteria. It is quite specific, it is clearly measurable in terms of delivery days, it is agreed and realistic and it is timed, the improvement to take place over a maximum 12-month period.

Having now added the strategy it is also clear how the objective is to be achieved, i.e. with the use of a new distribution system which takes advantage of the latest technology to control the order, stock and delivery system.

HAVING A CLEAR MISSION STATEMENT

The best way to quantify your business objectives is through a mission statement. Sometimes referred to as a vision statement, it will detail the whole point of your business. In many ways this is the hardest part of your business strategy to write because it must outline succinctly the whole thrust of your business.

The mission statement is also the most misunderstood part of the business planning process. Many people think that it should be couched in eloquent language and be full of lofty ideas for the business. All too often it becomes pompous, with little meaning and purpose because it is largely incomprehensible to those who read it.

> **TIP**
>
> Confine your mission statement to no more than one page and avoid waffle and statements that cannot be quantified.

The four key components of a mission statement:

◆ The **role or contribution** that the business makes – is it a voluntary organisation or a charity? Are you in business to supply goods and services and make a profit?
◆ A **definition** of the business – this should be given in terms of the benefits you provide or the needs that you satisfy. It should not define what you do or what you make. These should have been outlined as part of the first component.

◆ An outline of your **distinctive competencies** – the factors that differentiate your business from the competition. These will be the skills or capabilities you offer that are not, or cannot be, offered by your competitors.

◆ The **indications for the future** – what the business will do. What it might do in the future and what it will never do.

A good mission statement

A good mission statement is written in two parts. In the first part you outline the industry that you are in and the products that you offer. In simple clear terms, this will relate to exactly what your business does. The second part comprises the business strategies that you follow to achieve success. These can take any number of different forms, and some basic examples could include:

◆ We will provide an excellent service to all customers to achieve total satisfaction.

◆ We will accomplish high productivity levels through sound planning, organisation and teamwork.

◆ We will earn sufficient profits to ensure investment in new technology together with providing a good return to shareholders.

◆ We will earn high employee loyalty and motivation by showing respect for their capabilities and providing future training and development opportunities.

◆ We will gain recognition in the market for being a highly professional, ethical, quality-assured business.

Sample mission statement

Our mission statement concentrates on the four key components that we consider essential to our customers, our investors, our staff and the community in which we operate.

Our business

We aim to operate an ethical business in the financial services
sector offering products and services that provide value for money.

Quality to our customers

We value our customers as the foundation of our business. Our
relationships with customers and suppliers are based on principles
of respect and mutual benefit. We aim to develop profitable and
lasting relationships. We want to build on what we do well and to
innovate to meet changing customer needs.

Quality to our investors

We have a long-term responsibility to everyone who has a stake in
the business to operate with care, efficiency and, of prime
importance, at a profit.

Our objective is to earn the profits needed to provide a consistent
increase in the value of our shareholders' investment, obtain the
highest credit ratings and finance the ongoing development and
growth of our business.

Quality to our staff

We respect the experience and skills of our staff and value the
contribution that every person makes to the business team. We
recognise that pride and enjoyment in the job come from
commitment, leadership by example and accomplishment. Our goal
is to work together to reward, train and develop our staff in ways
that acknowledge performance and individual abilities.

Quality to the community

We recognise that our actions must acknowledge our responsibilities for the wellbeing and stability of the community as a whole. With this in mind we will aim to support the community through the involvement of our staff in voluntary roles, in addition to which we pledge to donate a contribution of 1% of our total profits to charitable causes.

SETTING MARKETING OBJECTIVES

When considering your marketing objectives, ensure that they are compatible with your overall business objectives as well as with the overall direction of your business.

There are four alternatives that any business has when establishing marketing objectives:

◆ Sell existing products to existing markets.
◆ Extend existing products into new markets.
◆ Develop new products for existing markets.
◆ Develop new products for new markets.

For a new business your choice may be limited to the latter two because you have no existing products. This will, of course, change over time and you need to be aware of the alternatives.

Marketing objectives could include:

◆ Increase product awareness in the target market by 10% over the next 12 months, such increase to be measured by customer surveys.

◆ Increase sales by 10% over the next 12 months by developing new markets in Europe for existing products.

One important point to consider when setting your marketing objectives is that they must not conflict; multiple objectives must be consistent with each other.

Avoid having too many marketing objectives. With too many you may find that, because you are trying to pull your business in so many different directions, a coherent strategy becomes impossible. This can lead to your financial resources becoming so stretched that none of your marketing objectives will be achieved.

4
Defining Your Business Strategy

To succeed in business it is essential to have a basic grasp of business strategy techniques. As the owner of your business you will be responsible for all aspects of running the business and entirely responsible for the strategic management of it. You will decide the strategy for your business and plan how that strategy is to be put into effect.

TIP

You must understand that strategic management is an ongoing process designed to help you stay ahead in business.

In its most basic form, strategic management has three clear components:

◆ analysis
◆ choice
◆ implementation.

Before taking any decision on strategy you need to assess where you are now and where you want to be (analysis). Then decide what options are available to you and evaluate those options in order to select an appropriate strategy (choice). Once you have decided on your strategy you need to translate that strategy into action (implementation).

STRATEGIC ANALYSIS

There are two distinct areas in relation to any business that require analysis:

◆ the environment
◆ the resources of the business.

ANALYSING THE ENVIRONMENT USING A PESTE ANALYSIS

There are many factors in the environment that could impact upon your business, and a PESTE analysis is designed to provide a focused framework for your research.

P – Political
E – Economic
S – Social
T – Technological
E – Environmental

Political

Political forces on a business may at first seem inconsequential, although more and more legislation is being enacted which has a direct impact on all businesses. You may need to consider, for example, health and safety legislation governing conditions in the workplace and consumer protection legislation covering labelling and packaging.

Ensure that you identify and comply with all relevant legislation. Failure to do so can be extremely costly in terms of fines or other penalties. (See Chapter 2.)

Economic

Economic forces include the effects of inflation, interest rates and exchange rates. With the development of the Single European Market, even if you do not export any goods or services you may face increasing competition from firms within Europe. This means that exchange rate movements can still be relevant, especially while the UK remains outside the Single European Currency.

Careful consideration must also be given to economic trends within the UK. For example, will rising interest rates affect the spending habits of your customers? Can increased costs be passed on or is your market price-sensitive?

Social

Social forces include the consideration of changing demographic trends in your customer base and the changing social climate in different parts of the country. Greater emphasis is now being placed on links between the business community and educational establishments to provide a greater understanding of business techniques to students. This could be a source of potential business opportunities.

Technological

Technological forces have been one of the most important aspects affecting businesses over the last decade. The development of information technology has affected the ways in which business is conducted, including the use of faxes and e-mail and not overlooking the opportunities created by the Internet.

Rapid advances in technology have presented all businesses with tremendous opportunities. The use of the latest available technology must be considered whatever your business.

Environmental

The final factor, environmental, is often dismissed as unnecessary by people on the basis that the whole point of this analysis is to look at the environment. I do not agree. The impact of a business on the environment must be considered quite separately. Some of the issues may overlap with the concerns relating to legislation but many – for example, the use of genetic engineering – are important enough to warrant an independent heading.

Completing an audit of resources

In the case of a new business you may have no existing resources to audit, but even at this stage you can think about the sort of resources that you may require as the business progresses. There are three key headings under which your resources will fall:

◆ physical
◆ human
◆ financial.

Physical resources

Your physical resources might fall under different sub-headings, for example, plant and machinery, tools and equipment, and vehicles. The assessment of your business's physical resources must not be just a straight list of what you physically have in this respect. You need to go one stage further and determine the exact nature of each resource in terms of age, condition, capability, location and, most importantly, how long it will last and when it will require replacement. This will enable you to make long-term plans for future capital investment.

Human resources

As with your physical resources, a mere list of the staff that you have, or propose to have in the future, is insufficient. You need to make an assessment of the skills of each individual together with an estimate of how adaptable they may be under changing circumstances.

For a new business you will need to consider carefully the skills that you require of any potential staff. We will look at this in some detail in Chapter 9 together with the implications of the various pieces of legislation which affect both you and your staff.

Financial resources

These will include all the sources of finance that you have, both from your own resources and borrowed funds. Within this audit you will also include the control of your debtors and creditors. The first is a use of funds, i.e. you are effectively lending them money, and the second is a source of funds, i.e. they are lending money to you.

For a new business, financial resources may be described in terms of what you need rather than what you actually have. It will give you an indication of the amount of funding that you are likely to require split in terms of your own contribution and the funding required from external sources.

STRATEGIC CHOICE

Having completed the audit and analysis, the next step in the strategic management process is evaluation of all of the available options. These should, of course, be evaluated on the basis of the business goals and objectives previously established.

This is the time to set aside any resistance to change, avoid all preconceptions and evaluate all of the options that you consider should contribute to the success of your business. The four-stage process outlined below will help.

Assess your options

There are four options available to any existing business:

◆ Withdraw from the market entirely.
◆ Consolidate the existing position within the market.
◆ Increase market penetration.
◆ Introduce new products or services.

Withdraw from the market entirely

Withdrawing from the market can mean a number of options.

1. Complete liquidation of the business.
2. Sale of the business to a competitor or a new management team.
3. Licensing or sub-contracting agreement.

The last option could arise if one part of the business was unprofitable on a stand-alone basis. But, if the work was to be sub-contracted it could make the overall business more economically viable.

Consolidate the existing position within the market

Consolidation is usually an internal business option where, for example, the business may concentrate on improving quality, efficiency and productivity. All of these actions would not necessarily increase the overall sales turnover, but they could have an effect on increased profitability.

Increase market penetration

Increasing market penetration would be an attempt to increase sales turnover by expanding into new markets for existing products or services. This could perhaps be achieved by exporting for the first time into new overseas markets. It could also include the potential take-over of similar competitors or collaboration with other businesses on joint ventures. This last option is becoming more and more popular, particularly involving joint ventures with businesses within the European Market.

Introduce new products or services

This can be achieved in a number of ways. Within the business there may be substantial research and development opportunities for existing products or services that can be modified or extended to be used in a different manner. Further options could include the take-over of businesses that offer alternative products, or you might be able to negotiate a licensing agreement to produce new products using your existing production capabilities.

> **TIP**
>
> There is another final option which is to do nothing. Obviously if you adopt this strategy you will achieve very little.

Decide whether the options are suitable for your business

The suitability of a particular option can be measured by the extent to which it fits the needs of your business, as identified using the SWOT analysis (which will be looked at in detail in Chapter 6). Using the four key elements the selected option should either:

◆ build on a strength
◆ resolve a weakness
◆ exploit an opportunity

or

◆ avoid a threat.

> **TIP**
>
> In some cases an option that is suitable is the only one that can be implemented, despite reservations about whether it is feasible or acceptable.

For example, does this option capitalise on your business strengths, overcome or avoid weaknesses or counter potential threats? Naturally, it should fit in with your overall business objectives.

Assess the feasibility of the option

Assessment of the feasibility of an option is primarily concerned with whether or not it can be implemented. An option that seeks to break into a new market might be suitable in terms of achieving a perceived opportunity, but lack of resources could render it unfeasible.

There are a number of fundamental questions that need to be considered when assessing the feasibility of an option. Consider the following examples:

◆ Is this option capable of being funded? Does the business have sufficient internal resources, or, if outside funding is required, is this likely to be obtained?
◆ Can the business perform to the required level? Does the business have the capability of increasing productivity or quality standards?
◆ Can the necessary market position be achieved? Does the business have sufficient marketing skills to increase sales turnover in potential new markets?
◆ Are the required skills available within the business? Do you have the required business skills to compete in new markets, or will additional human resources be required? If new staff are required, where will they come from and what skills will they need?
◆ Can the necessary materials or services be obtained? Will the suppliers be able to meet the increased demand for raw materials, and if so, on what terms will these be supplied?

These questions are only some examples.

Consider whether the option is acceptable

To whom should these options be acceptable? The simple answer is that they have to be acceptable to the stakeholders within the business.

There are many definitions of stakeholders, but in this instance they are considered to be the owners of the business together with potential or existing investors.

If funding is being sought, it is of paramount importance to the potential investors that the chosen options are acceptable, otherwise they will not invest. The questions of suitability and feasibility are of secondary importance.

When considering options for acceptability, give additional consideration to the following factors:

◆ The selected option must increase the profitability of the business. The reason for this is that if an outside investor is to consider investing, the business must generate additional income to pay for the investment either in terms of interest or dividends.

◆ The element of risk will be of prime importance to a prospective investor. They need to be convinced that the amount of risk they are taking by investing in the business is minimised and that not only will their investment be safe, but that they will also receive an appropriate reward.

◆ A key measure of the acceptability of an option is gained following an assessment of the returns that are likely to accrue to all stakeholders as a result of that option being adopted.

◆ Clearly define the capital structure of the business from the outset, recognising the individual investment made by each party. This applies in all cases where there is more than one owner, for example, a new partner is being sought, or shares in a limited company are being offered in exchange for investment.

For some entrepreneurs, the question of
relinquishing part ownership of their business
is very emotive. In many cases there is a failure
to recognise that by allowing an investor part
ownership, the investor's commitment for the
business to be a success can also increase.

> **TIP**
>
> Part ownership of a thriving successful business is a better investment than total ownership, and control of a failing business.

STRATEGIC IMPLEMENTATION

There are two distinct aspects of implementation that you need to
consider. You need to plan carefully how you are going to do it before
you can actually carry out the necessary tasks to implement the
strategy. There are three key areas into which you can break down the
implementation process:

◆ planning and allocation of resources
◆ the structure of the business
◆ management of the people and systems in the business.

Planning and allocation of resources

Earlier in this chapter we looked at the resources of the business under
three distinct headings:

◆ physical
◆ human
◆ financial.

For a new business it will be relatively easy for you to plan what
resources you need and then allocate them successfully. For a growing
business, however, the process can be slightly more complicated. This
is where it is essential that forward planning is undertaken. You may
also like to consider the position if your business is in decline. In these

circumstances your resource problems will centre on what to do with those that are excess to requirements.

It will be easy to plan and allocate the resources under the first two headings, physical and human. You should have clearly established exactly what equipment and other assets you will require, together with the staff that you need to run the business. Financial resources, however, are more difficult to plan and allocate, especially if you have to raise funds from external sources.

This is where financial forecasting is absolutely essential and should have been in place right from the inception of your business. Unless you plan your finances correctly you could find yourself short of cash and, despite the fact that your business may be thriving, this could mean failure. (Financial forecasting is looked at in some detail in Chapter 13.)

> **TIP**
>
> Just because you have sufficient resources to start your business does not mean that you do not need to plan properly. Fail to plan and you plan to fail.

The structure of your business

For a new business the structure is likely to be uncomplicated. The owner will undertake the responsibilities of management and either run the business by themselves or perhaps, depending on the type of business, have one or two other staff. If, however, the business grows, this structure will no longer operate effectively and some of the tasks of management may need to be delegated.

This may also be the case if the owner of the business does not have some of the skills necessary to run their business from the outset. The most common example in this respect is the financial records that the business must keep. Where the owner has perhaps neither the time, nor the expertise to undertake this task, it is preferable to delegate this to a part-time book-keeper. It is vital, however, that even where this task is delegated, the owner of the business must retain overall control of the finances.

Management of the people and systems in the business

If you are going to employ staff in your business it is vitally important that you have strategies in place to manage them successfully. In addition, you must have clear control and information systems in place if you are going to redefine your business strategy at any point in the future.

> **TIP**
>
> Keep the structure of your business under constant review. As your business grows do not be afraid to delegate responsibility. You must concentrate your efforts on what you do best.

Managing your staff

There are a number of key considerations that you will need to think about when planning how you are going to manage your staff. Some of these include:

◆ What do you want them to do?
◆ How do you want them to do it?
◆ When do you want them to do it?
◆ How much are you going to pay them?
◆ What hours should they work?
◆ What training will you provide?

The list is not complete and if you are going to gain the most benefit from your staff there is one important question you need to consider – how will you motivate them? Unless they are motivated in their work they will not perform at their best for you.

Control and information systems

To succeed in business you must have some form of management information system in place to help you control your business. Some knowledge of how your business is performing will also help with defining future strategy. The five key areas in which you need some form of system to aid you are:

◆ financial performance analysis
◆ ongoing market analysis
◆ sales and distribution analysis
◆ physical resource analysis
◆ human resource analysis.

At this stage I do not propose to say anything further about the management information systems you will require to cover the analysis of your business performance. This subject is covered in detail in Chapter 23.

STRATEGIC THREATS TO CONSIDER

It is relevant to look at some of the threats that you may encounter in the competitive world of business. Broadly speaking, these can be categorised under the following headings:

◆ the threat posed by new entrants into the market
◆ the threat of substitute products
◆ the power of suppliers and buyers
◆ the extent of competitive rivalry.

New entrants

In starting your business you will, of course, fall into this category. You will need to consider carefully how you are to overcome any barriers to entry into the market. These will differ depending on both the industry and the market. Examples could include:

◆ significant economies of scale and associated cost savings
◆ large initial capital expenditure requirement
◆ restricted access to distribution channels
◆ established brand presence in the market.

One way to counter a barrier to entering the market is through differentiation. Consider how the increasing use of the Internet has enabled many small businesses to compete with large businesses on an equal basis.

> **TIP**
>
> If there are any barriers to entry into your chosen market you will need to have clear strategies in place to deal with them if you are going to compete effectively.

Substitute products

In any market there is always the danger that substitute products could be introduced. Consider as an example the market for soft drinks. New entrants into the cola market in recent years have included own brand products by some of the large retailers.

It is open to question whether such products have actually had any effect on a market which is dominated by two major players, Coca Cola and Pepsi. On the other hand, the substitute products in the market for sugar – sweeteners – have achieved some success due perhaps to the move towards a healthier lifestyle.

You will need to consider the extent of the threat any substitute product may be to your own product. As part of your strategy you may need to minimise the risks of such substitution, by possibly extending your own product range.

The power of suppliers and buyers

TIP

Make sure you are aware of the implications of the Competition Act 1998 which imposes severe penalties for over-charging or any form of price fixing.

You must never underestimate the power of suppliers and buyers in the market. A sole supplier of a particular product will be in a strong position to influence prices and this could impact upon your profit margins. In effect, they could dictate the selling price of the goods that you purchase from them.

Buyer power can also have an impact upon your profit margins. The grocery market is an example. With the vast majority of such goods being sold through major supermarkets, the grocery suppliers have found their margins being squeezed. The supermarkets needed to offer their products at the lowest possible price to the consumer in order to compete with each other. To do this, they introduced own label or own packed items and effectively dictated quality standards and prices.

The dilemma for the grocery producers was whether to meet the demands of the supermarkets or to find alternative outlets for their products. With large-scale production, however, finding an alternative market was not a viable option and the grocery suppliers have had to achieve cost savings of their own in order to stay in business.

TIP

Never rely on one customer for your sales. The less customers you have the more power they are likely to have over your business.

Competitive rivalry

As part of the strategic analysis of the market you will need to investigate the degree of rivalry between competitors. You can be sure that in any market there will be competitive rivalry.

Consider, for example, the market for home electrical appliances. In any high street you can be sure that there will be a number of suppliers all offering virtually the same goods at similar prices. It would be an understatement to say that the competitive rivalry in this market is intense. It also gives a further example of the power of buyers. The major high street suppliers of electrical goods have extensive purchasing power over the manufacturers.

> **TIP**
>
> Competitive rivalry will exist in every market – make sure that you have an appropriate strategy to differentiate your business from your competitors'.

5

Obtaining the Right Support

There is a substantial amount of assistance available to small businesses. If you enter the term 'Business Support' into any Internet search engine, and refine your search to UK sites only, you will probably receive in excess of 300,000 suggested sites. Unfortunately a great deal of this help is missed purely through ignorance of the actual scheme. Certainly with respect to grants or subsidies the business or project must not be started until confirmation has been received that the funds have been awarded.

Some people also do not seem to wish to discuss their plans to establish a new business and so they can never receive appropriate help and advice. Only by seeking help at a very early change can you optimise the assistance that you will receive.

The number of schemes available across the UK are wide and diverse and offer both financial and non-financial assistance. In this chapter we will look at non-financial assistance. Grants and subsidies that are available to businesses will be looked at in Chapter 14. Different schemes also apply across the country so you will need to undertake your own investigation to see what is available to you locally. For this reason, and as a general guide, I will outline in this chapter the assistance that is available to businesses in my own location, the North East of England.

> **TIP**
>
> If you are thinking of starting a business then your local Business Link or equivalent should be your first port of call before you do anything else.

The Small Business Service was established to help small businesses and to represent their interests across Government. It works closely with the network of Business Links in England, Business Shops in Scotland, Business Connect in Wales and EDnet in Northern Ireland.

BUSINESS LINKS

Business Links and the other support organisations throughout the UK provide a wide variety of advice and guidance to businesses, most of which is entirely free of charge. Examples include help with:

◆ design and production of business cards and stationery
◆ advice on putting together your business plan
◆ guidance on market research and strategy for your proposed business
◆ how to raise money for growth
◆ how to locate suppliers
◆ information on legislation or regulations that could affect your business.

Some of these take the form of training courses and others, such as design work, are undertaken by experienced professionals employed on a consultancy basis. In most cases, this support is offered free of charge.

Support is also available through these organisations on a subsidised basis where accredited consultants are employed to assist you and their fee is only partly payable by you. In Tyne and Wear for instance a 50% grant of up to £2,000 is available towards the costs of employing a professional to design your website.

Business Links services

In addition to the general advice and guidance that Business Links offer they also have a number of key services:

◆ comprehensive business information service providing detailed and specific research

◆ personal and reliable advice from an allocated independent Personal Business Advisor (PBA)

◆ events, promotions, seminars and conferences on business-related topics which also provide networking opportunities with other business owners.

Each Business Link will also have a number of specialists who are independently accredited to work with small businesses and who are employed on a freelance basis. This is one of the areas in which I work. I am independently accredited by the British Accreditation Bureau and contracted by Business Links to provide consultancy support to businesses, primarily on strategic planning, fund raising and marketing.

> **TIP**
>
> Consultancy support may be available to you totally free of charge. In some cases the fee that I charge businesses is paid fully by Business Links.

ENTERPRISE AGENCIES

Enterprise Agencies are not-for-profit organisations that provide advice, counselling, information, training and practical help to businesses. Enterprise Agencies often work in partnership with other business support organisations such as Business Links. Their main aim is to help small businesses start up and grow.

Training facilities

Most Enterprise Agencies offer training seminars in-house in a range of subjects relevant to small businesses. Depending on the financial support that the Agency receives, either from government or private sponsorship, the courses will either be free of charge or available on payment of a nominal fee.

Other services

Enterprise Agencies can also offer a range of
other services. These may include help with
innovation and technology issues, and
information on importing and exporting
including assistance with finding overseas
partners. In some cases they can also offer
subsidised work space on easy rental terms.
Secretarial and other administrative support may also be available.

THE BRITISH CHAMBERS OF COMMERCE

The Member Chambers of the British Chambers of Commerce (BCC)
are subject to tough accreditation criteria to ensure that they offer the
very best in business support. Membership of an individual Chamber
can, however, be expensive and the actual cost is defined by the size of
your business. The BCC do offer a number of services to members
quite apart from campaigning on behalf of members in both local and
central government concerns.

Information and events

Information and advice on all aspects of running a business is
available. The individual Chambers organise a number of networking
events and conferences throughout the year.

Training

Collectively, the British Chambers of Commerce are the largest single
provider of training in the UK, delivering in excess of 7,500 courses
each year for over 110,000 people from businesses of all sizes.

Export assistance

The individual Chambers operate schemes to assist with export opportunities and can offer help with arranging attendance at trade missions and fairs throughout the world. They also provide a range of international trade services. These include:

◆ guidance on overseas marketing
◆ advice and information on the shipment of goods
◆ methods of obtaining payment
◆ how to issue the correct export documentation.

TIP

You will need to weigh up carefully the costs of joining a Chamber of Commerce against the likely benefits for your business.

Cost savings

Taking advantage of their bulk purchasing power, the BCC negotiate exclusive deals with national suppliers to offer members generous savings on high quality business services.

THE FEDERATION OF SMALL BUSINESSES

The Federation of Small Businesses (FSB) is the largest campaigning pressure group which works to promote and protect the interests of the self-employed and small businesses. The FSB was formed in 1974 and is non-profit-making and non-party-political. Membership fees are based on a sliding scale according to whether you are a sole trader and on the number of employees you have.

Free services to members

The FSB offers a number of free services to members including:

◆ telephone helplines
◆ export information and guidance

- legal assistance – both personal and business-related
- advice with taxation, VAT, PAYE, employment law and health and safety.

The FSB also offers businesses legal and professional insurance and assistance with defending legal action brought under a number of Acts of Parliament, together with other claims made against a business.

Legal and professional insurance
The FSB offers businesses legal and professional insurance of up to £1,000,000 to protect business activities against:

- Inland Revenue investigations
- VAT tribunals and appeals
- industrial tribunal costs
- employment disputes
- statutory sick pay audits
- PAYE audits.

Defending legal action
The FSB will help with defending against prosecution in connection with:

- Health and Safety at Work Act
- Consumer Protection Act
- Food Safety Act
- Statutory Licence
- Data Protection Act
- damage to property
- personal injury.

TIP

Membership of the FSB can be very cost effective – contact the head office for details of your local regional membership secretary.

SHELL LIVEWIRE

Shell *Live*WIRE is a UK-wide Shell Investment Programme. It aims to develop and manage programmes that improve the opportunities for young people wishing to start or develop their own business. *Live*WIRE is available to any 16 to 30 year old in the UK who is looking to receive free local advice and support.

The Outreach Programme

The aim of this programme is to act as a gateway to youth enterprise support. Every person who makes an enquiry receives a 'Start your own business' booklet. This helps them to understand what starting a business involves and shows how to turn a business idea or a potential business idea into reality. If appropriate, a suitable business advisor can be appointed who can provide further business support material.

Business start-up awards

*Live*WIRE operates an annual awards scheme at county, regional and national levels with the national winners competing in an overall UK final. Entrants must meet the age criteria and have been trading for not less than three months and not more than 18 months. Entry is gained by submitting a business plan to a local co-ordinator, which is then passed to an independent judging panel for assessment against *Live*WIRE guidelines.

TIP

Winning an award can provide new opportunities for your business – if you qualify you have nothing to lose by submitting your entry.

In addition to the above, regional and national awards are made in recognition of young businesses that have demonstrated significant progress in the first few years since starting up. The awards are both financial and non-financial and can represent significant sums or substantial support in kind.

THE FORUM OF PRIVATE BUSINESS

The Forum of Private Business (FPB) is a campaigning business support organisation. Founded in 1977, the FPB serves its members as a non-partisan non-profit-making organisation. Apart from offering representations on their behalf, the FPB gives members the ability to search an extensive Member Information Service database. This provides details of member concerns on such matters as banking, VAT, taxation and employment.

Representation

The FPB operates a unique ballot system which gives members direct influence on the laws and policies affecting them. The FPB collates these opinions and provides regular representations and evidence to the decision-makers in European, national and local government. In addition, representations are made to Financial Institutions about concerns relating to the profitability of businesses that could be affected by the decisions of such institutions.

Profit advantage schemes

The FPB helps businesses to maximise profits by reducing costs through unique profit builders. These are do-it-yourself tools which help to manage such issues as late-payment, statutory sick pay, banking and insurance. It can also help reduce the cost of utilities through the Utility Discount Group, which includes gas, electricity, telephone and mobile telephone services.

> **TIP**
>
> The savings that you could make from the Utility Discount Group scheme should be more than sufficient to warrant becoming a member – the FPB claim that the average saving per member is £600.

Campaigns

At any one time, the FPB is campaigning actively to bring about benefits to the small business community. In recent years such campaigns have included:

◆ lobbying for fairer business rents and rates

◆ trying to improve the services available to small businesses from banks

◆ amending the legislation on insolvency rules.

The FPB also provides members with 'Action Alerts' which give advance warning and advice to businesses on the effects of forthcoming legislation changes.

LAWYERS FOR YOUR BUSINESS

Lawyers For Your Business is designed for all types of business whether you are just starting, already running, or indeed are a substantial enterprise. Lawyers participating in the scheme offer a number of services:

◆ A free consultation with a solicitor – this should be of at least half an hour.

◆ Free diagnosis – the solicitor will tell you what further help you need, if any, and the likely costs.

◆ No obligation – whatever advice the solicitor gives, you are not under any commitment to take the matter further.

There are no restrictions on who can use the scheme, which is available through some 1,700 solicitors throughout England and Wales. To find the nearest participating solicitor you should contact Lawyers For Your Business at The Law Society.

> **TIP**
>
> Things can and do go wrong with some business transactions. Proper legal advice at an early stage could stop small problems becoming large problems.

6
Researching the Market

Research and analysis of your potential market are crucial to your success. Unless you understand what is happening in the market and the trends and desires of the consumers, you cannot fulfil the basic requirement of marketing. You must be able to satisfy and anticipate the demands of the consumer.

Without customers you will not survive. Unless you can establish who your customers are, how much they will pay and where they will buy from, you cannot formulate a successful marketing strategy.

There are six questions that you need to answer:
◆ Who are your potential customers?
◆ What do they buy?
◆ Why do they buy the products that they buy?
◆ How much influence do others have on the purchase decision?
◆ When do they buy?
◆ Where do they buy?

Customers could come from a narrow or broad segment of the total population. They can be segmented into a wide variety of headings, such as:

◆ age bands
◆ occupations
◆ standard of education
◆ income levels

- family position, i.e. married, single and with or without children
- location.

SEGMENTING THE POTENTIAL MARKET

There are a number of different ways in which you can segment your customers and the market. From the outset you should be clear, however, that there is no one perfect method of segmentation.

Geographic segmentation

This is one of the simplest forms of segmentation. It consists of dividing your market on the basis of the geographical location of your customers. If all your sales are made in the domestic market, i.e. within the UK, you could segment your customers by region. On an international basis, you may consider that different countries have different consumer trends and can be segmented accordingly.

Demographic segmentation

These forms of segmentation are probably the most popular, largely because they are associated with differences in consumer demand. This type of segmentation involves identifying consumers by socio-economic factors such as age, sex, family size, income or lifestyle. It is also one of the easiest to undertake with the wealth of information available from both central and local government statistics.

There are two main methods used to provide the socio-economic groupings. The first classifies occupation and social class groups. The second, ACORN, classifies types of neighbourhoods.

Occupation and social class segmentation

Social Class	Occupation
A	Higher managerial
B	Intermediate management
C1	Supervisory/ lower management
C2	Skilled manual
D	Semi-skilled/ unskilled
E	Lowest level of subsistence

Care, however, should be taken when making general assumptions about a segment that is based upon one single social class. People with high incomes, perhaps in social class B, may have little disposable income as they may also have high fixed expenditure, such as a mortgage, which would leave little money left for 'luxury' products.

ACORN segmentation

ACORN is the acronym for 'A Classification Of Residential Neighbourhoods', which analyses households on the basis of the type of property. The information for this system is derived from the UK population census conducted every ten years, the latest in 2001.

The ACORN system is based on the assumption that consumer behaviour and lifestyles are closely related to neighbourhood types, and there is strong evidence to support this assumption. ACORN has proved useful in the compilation of direct mailing lists.

ACORN main classification headings

A	Modern family housing for manual workers
B	Modern family housing for higher incomes
C	Older housing of intermediate status
D	Very poor quality, older terraced housing
E	Rural areas
F	Urban local authority housing
G	Housing with most overcrowding
H	Low income areas with immigrants
I	Students and high status non-family areas
J	Traditional high status suburbia
K	Areas of elderly people

TIP

Each of these groups can be identified by post code which can be used to provide a precise geographic location for each demographic segment.

Product segmentation

In essence, product segmentation is used to identify those consumers who purchase a particular product and those who do not. There will, of course, be segments of the market that will never have the need for a particular product. Similarly, there will be consumers who may offer potential opportunities in the future.

Benefit and lifestyle segmentation

This takes demographic segmentation one stage further by linking the lifestyle of consumers to their decision to purchase a particular product. Consider the market for toiletries. All brands of toothpaste offer the same basic benefit – they clean your teeth.

How then do manufacturers differentiate their products in the market? The answer relates to the benefits that the product offers. Generally, toothpastes concentrate their marketing on the flavour of the product, the avoidance of tooth decay or making teeth whiter. All these differences will appeal to different segments of the consumer market.

THE IMPORTANCE OF COMPETITIVE ADVANTAGE

Competitive advantage is critical to your marketing. You must offer some form of differentiation from other businesses in the same market if you are to persuade consumers to buy from you. Competitive advantage can take two main forms:

◆ **Financial** – either through efficiency savings which lead to lower costs of production and/or a lower selling price to the consumer.
◆ **Differentiation in service** – perhaps through longer opening hours, an improved delivery service, a measurable difference in the quality of service or a higher quality product.

There is, of course, a further option – combining both of the above forms. However, there is a danger that trying to be competitive on all fronts could result in a mixed message being sent to consumers.

TIP

Your competitive advantage does not have to be complicated. It does, however, need to be highly visible and recognised by your customers.

Looking at the competition

Understanding your competitors is crucial if you are to obtain a competitive advantage. Only in this way can you exploit the opportunities available to you and counter the prospective threats.

Competition will come in four different ways:
◆ **Direct** – generated by businesses that offer the same products or services as you in the same market.

◆ **Indirect** – businesses that although operating in different markets and with different products may pose a threat if they can easily diversify into your market.

◆ **Industry** – businesses that operate in the same product area but which sell in different markets.

◆ **Linked** – businesses that offer the same service but deliver in a different manner.

The importance of identification

It is extremely important for you to have as much information on your competitors as possible. If you do not know who your competitors are, and what they are doing, there is little prospect of your being able to compete.

Establish who they are – Full details of the business, where they are located, what products or services they offer, who they sell their products to and at what price.

Identify their marketing objectives – Are they trying to expand their market share in the existing market, or are they expanding into new markets? What product portfolio do they have? Is it static or are they introducing new products?

Analyse their marketing strategies – Are they concentrating on a particular market segment? What promotional strategies do they use? Are they innovative in their approach to the market? Are they seen as market leaders, or are they happy to follow the lead of others?

> **TIP**
>
> When you assess your competitors – be totally honest. You only fool yourself otherwise.

Look at whether they have any strengths and weaknesses – What is their competitive advantage? Do they have a strong brand image? What weaknesses could you exploit?

USING A SWOT ANALYSIS

SWOT is the acronym for Strengths, Weaknesses, Opportunities and Threats. A SWOT analysis encourages you to think about the positive sides of your business as well as the negative aspects. It should also be used to assess your competition.

A SWOT analysis is compiled using a grid to enable you to consider how you will match your strengths to your opportunities and how you will overcome your weaknesses and threats. The strengths and opportunities are listed in the columns on the left and are represented by existing or potential assets. The weaknesses and threats are listed in the columns on the right and these are represented by existing or potential liabilities.

Strengths

Something that you are doing correctly or are good at. It may be a skill, a competence, or a competitive advantage that you have over your rivals.

Questions to ask:

◆ What are my advantages?
◆ What is it that I do well?

Weaknesses

Something that compared to your rivals you lack or do poorly. A condition that puts you at a disadvantage.

Questions to ask:

◆ What could be improved?
◆ What is it that I do badly?
◆ What should be avoided?

Opportunities

A realistic avenue for future growth in the business. Something to be used to develop a competitive advantage.

Questions to ask:

◆ What are the market trends?
◆ How can they be exploited?
◆ What chances are there for me?

Threats

A factor that you may, or may not have control over that could lead to a decline in business.

Questions to ask:

◆ What is my competition doing?
◆ What obstacles do I face?
◆ What effect will a new entrant have on my market?

It is important that you understand that your products or services could fall within different segments of the SWOT analysis. Some will be seen as strengths or opportunities for your business. Others will be weaknesses or threats when compared to your competitors.

ESTABLISHING YOUR UNIQUE SELLING POINT

A unique selling point, or USP, is a crucial element in defining your competitive advantage. You must establish what it is that makes you different from your competitors. Having identified these advantages, you must use them in your marketing.

When identifying your unique selling points there are five questions that you need to ask yourself:

◆ Will the customers in the market perceive this as an advantage?
◆ Is it significantly different from what my competitors are offering?
◆ Will my customers actually believe in this USP?
◆ Will my customers receive some benefit from this USP?
◆ Will this USP motivate customers sufficiently to make a purchase?

An advantage must offer clear benefits, perhaps better quality or better value. The key is significant benefit to the customer. Your products or services may have numerous features, but unless they offer real benefits there is little incentive for your customers to purchase them.

The important point to try to focus on is that your competitive advantages must be sustainable. It is essential therefore, when you are setting your objectives based on competitive advantage, that you also consider cost effectiveness and overall profitability. To establish the relationship between benefits to the customer as opposed to the costs to you, you should consider these four alternative scenarios:

◆ low cost to you – low benefit to your customers
◆ high cost to you – low benefit to your customers
◆ low cost to you – high benefit to your customers
◆ high cost to you – high benefit to your customers.

It should be obvious that the competitive advantages which are most cost effective to you, whilst at the same time offering high benefits to your customers, should be the ones on which you concentrate your marketing efforts.

> **TIP**
>
> If you cannot identify any competitive advantage offered by your existing products or services then you need to improve them so that you can.

DEFINING YOUR CRITICAL SUCCESS FACTORS

Within all markets there are a number of factors that will be critical to your success. If you are to succeed you must therefore address these factors when formulating your strategy. Under normal circumstances, the number of critical success factors will not normally exceed five, although you must understand that there could be secondary factors that will contribute to your success.

All of these critical success factors should have already been established during your research and it is now time to prioritise them. Examples of critical success factors could include:

◆ delivery times
◆ speed of service

◆ quality of the product

◆ competitive pricing.

In many ways, these will also link up with the competitive advantages that you have established. It is important that once you have defined the factors critical to your success you then measure your own performance in these factors relative to your competitors.

The way to do this is to weight each factor out of a total score of 100 in terms of how critical it is. You then allocate a score out of ten for your own performance and that of your competitors. It is vitally important that you be totally objective when allocating a score. As an example, you may consider that there are three critical success factors. The first is weighted at 50, the second at 30, and the third at 20.

Once you have allocated a weighting to the factor you then multiply that weighting by the score that you have allocated for performance. This will then give you a total score that can be used as a measure of success.

		Your	Performance	Competitor	Performance
CSF	Weighting	Score	Measure	Score	Measure
1	50	8	400	7	350
2	30	5	150	7	210
3	20	6	120	5	100
	100	19	670	19	660

As you can see from the above example, on the basis of the pure scores that have been allocated, you and your competitor are exactly the same. However, taking the weighting of the factors into account, you have a marginal competitive advantage. If you find that you are scoring yourself low on the most important factors and high on the least important factors, then you obviously need to adopt a strategy that will improve your score on the most important factors. Using this system will help you concentrate your efforts and therefore your strategy on what your customers consider to be important.

Critical success factors will vary from industry to industry and from market to market. There can be no clear formula as to what will be most important for you. You will have to draw on the results of your research and establish your strategy in order to focus on the factors that are critical to your business.

TIP

You must work constantly to improve your score in all of the critical success factors that you have defined.

7

Identifying Your Products

Your products are the most important element of your business. Without products, you have nothing to sell and therefore have no market or customers. Even if you only have one product, in order to succeed you must still target that product into the right market. You must also continue to develop and enhance that product in order to meet the changing demands of the market.

As part of that development you will need to take decisions on quality, features and benefits, together with branding and packaging. Some of these decisions will, of course, also overlap into your decisions on promotion techniques considered in Chapter 11.

USING THE BOSTON CONSULTING GROUP (BCG) MATRIX

The Boston Consulting Group was established in the 1960s specifically to provide strategic marketing advice. As a result of their research they developed a matrix that analysed the product portfolio of a business in relation to the market.

This matrix classifies products according to cash usage and cash generation compared with relative market share and growth rate.

The BCG Matrix

'Star' products

These have a high market share and high growth rate.

They also generate a large cash inflow although this is fully offset by the cash they require for production.

'Cash Cow' products

These have a high market share although a low potential growth rate.

They generate a high cash inflow against minimal cash required for production.

'Question Mark' products

These have a high growth rate although they only have a low market share.

Cash generated is minimal against cash used, the net cashflow is negative.

'Dog' products

These have a low market share and low potential growth rate.

They generate minimal cash inflow which is fully matched by the cash they require for production.

From the above you can see that following introduction into the market, your products will move through a cycle represented in chronological order by 'Dog', 'Question Marks', 'Stars', and then 'Cash Cows'. The cash generated by the 'Cash Cows' is used to invest in the 'Stars' and a select few from the 'Question Marks'.

It is important that you also understand the potential dangers of misusing the BCG matrix. When conducting your product audit, you may find that a large number of products are in low growth markets, i.e. 'Dog' products. It is essential, therefore, that you establish the relationship that this product has within the overall market.

It may be that one such product was the initial product introduced by you that established your brand name and reputation in the market. It would be very unwise to remove that product from your product range, even if it does now only have a low market share. It is likely that if it is a manufactured product it will share the same production and distribution facilities with other new products. As such, despite the low market share, it will still remain a profitable product.

There are also limitations in using the BCG matrix as the sole form of analysis.

◆ Only two factors, market share and market growth, are taken into consideration but this can over-simplify the position.

◆ Cash flow rather than profitability is used to measure performance.

◆ Classification of individual products can be difficult.

◆ Products can move very quickly from one segment to another.

◆ It does not cater for the introduction of new products.

◆ It does not deal with markets that are experiencing decline.

> **TIP**
>
> Take care when you classify your products with the BCG matrix – some may not fall into one distinct section, they may be part-way between two.

The BCG matrix can be a very powerful tool to aid your product planning, especially if you link it together with the life cycle concept. This will give the matrix a new dimension and bring together the key components of products and markets.

THE PRODUCT LIFE CYCLE CONCEPT

This concept is based on the assumption that products are similar to all life forms and therefore have a finite time in the market. This means that from the initial development and introduction phase the product will experience a period of growth. It then enters a period of maturity until it starts to decline and eventually die.

The Product Life Cycle Concept

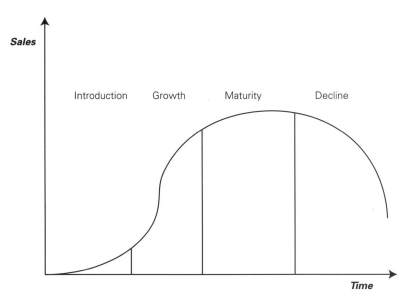

The amount of time in which a product moves through the cycle can be extremely variable. Some products will have a long life and others, perhaps those that can best be described as 'fads' or 'crazes', may have a very limited life.

TIP

There are some markets, particularly those in the basic essentials of life such as foodstuffs, where the product life cycle concept does not apply.

Linking the Product Life Cycle to the market

Using a simple framework you can link together the product life cycle to the market conditions you are likely to encounter at each individual stage. This will also give you an indication of the potential profitability in addition to the probable effect upon your cashflow.

	Introduction	Growth	Maturity	Decline
Market Growth	Uncertain	High	Slow	Contracting
Competition	Very few	Increasing	Strong	Declining
Sales	Low	Rapid growth	Peak with high share	Contracting if low share
Profits	Marginal	Depends on strategy	Peak and declining	Low
Cash flow	Negative	Building	High	Low

USING THE PRODUCT LIFE CYCLE FOR PRODUCT DEVELOPMENT

By combining the product life cycle with the BCG matrix you can formulate a strategy for product development. Ideally you will want to have a range of products within your portfolio, all of which are at different stages in the life cycle process.

A product's position within the life cycle is determined by a number of factors including:

◆ market growth rate
◆ potential for further market growth
◆ the number of competitors
◆ the spread of market share among competitors
◆ any barriers for entry into the market.

Only by considering all of the market factors can the position of the product be established within the life cycle. You must also remember that not all products will have the same life cycle profile. In addition, not all products will enter a decline phase. They may become 'necessities' and as such will always be required in one form or another. They may, however, require refinement in some way in order to stay ahead of other similar competitors.

The main point to remember is that you must have a range of products with the mature, profitable products producing cash for further product development. This means that you must be able to identify those products that in life cycle terms are at the mature stage, and in BCG matrix terms are 'Cash Cows'.

In terms of product development you have two basic choices:

◆ proactive product development
◆ reactive product development.

Proactive product development

This is a very risky option. You will be introducing brand new products and there is therefore a high risk of failure. Balancing that risk, however, is the high reward that could be achieved. If you are the first company to develop a new product and the market is receptive to you, you could quickly gain a high share of the new market. This would make it difficult for any other competitors to enter the market unless they had a better product. This, of course, could take them some time to produce.

Reactive product development

For obvious reasons, this strategy carries a substantially reduced risk. You are letting others lead the way and subsequently take all the risk. Only at the point when you can see that the new product is in demand will you attempt effectively to copy the competition. Having said that, you obviously need to ensure that you do not impinge on any patent or other legal protection that may have been registered. If you are fast enough, and can offer some extra innovation to the original product, you stand a good chance of being just as well placed in the market as the original introducer.

USING THE ANSOFF MATRIX TO CONSIDER PRODUCTS AND MARKETS

The Ansoff matrix defines two key factors for marketing – what is sold and who it is sold to. It therefore relates only to products and markets and gives you four alternative courses of action:

◆ selling existing products to existing markets
◆ extending existing products into new markets
◆ developing new products for existing markets
◆ developing new products for new markets.

These four options are set out in a four-box matrix that plots your existing and potential products against your existing and potential markets as follows:

	Present Products	New Products
Present Markets	Market Penetration	Product Development
New Markets	Market Extension	Diversification

◆ **Market penetration** – increasing the existing share in the existing market to facilitate further growth.
◆ **Market extension** – taking existing products into new markets, for example expanding sales from purely the domestic market into the European market.
◆ **Product development** – offering new products or modifying existing products into the existing markets.
◆ **Diversification** – either with related products and markets or unrelated products that are totally unconnected with the existing products and markets.

You can now start thinking about your marketing objectives by using the Ansoff matrix in conjunction with the analysis of your products that you completed in the life cycle analysis. You can also consider your markets using the Ansoff matrix in conjunction with the BCG matrix.

TARGETING THE RIGHT PRODUCT INTO THE RIGHT MARKET

Using the Ansoff matrix you will understand that you only have four choices to make concerning products and markets. What you need to consider is the element of risk in each proposed option. For example, introducing new products into new markets would carry a significantly higher risk than expanding existing products into existing markets. The degree of risk involved will also be affected by two other factors:

◆ How new the product is.
◆ How new the market is.

Existing products into existing markets

The overall aim of this strategy is to increase the market penetration of your products. In a naturally growing market this could be relatively easy, but where the market is effectively saturated or static this could be much more difficult. In a static market you will need to improve your competitive position by, for example, improving the quality of the product.

This strategy can also be beneficial in increasing profits in the short-term. When compared to the BCG matrix, the products most likely to succeed will be the 'Cash Cows' and the 'Stars'. This strategy also carries the lowest level of risk.

Existing products into new markets

Often referred to as market development, this strategy carries the next level of risk. Whilst retaining the relative security of the existing market for your products, it is an attempt to expand the business by entering new markets. The most obvious example is exporting for the first time.

As an alternative, during the course of segmenting the market you may have identified different market segments for your products. It is also possible that, if you have previously concentrated on a small local geographic area expansion can be achieved on a national basis.

New products into existing markets

Next on the scale of risk comes product development. This takes the form of either brand new products or the modification of existing products to meet the changing demands of the market. A good example is the development in personal computers over the last ten years. Virtually as soon as one product in this market is introduced it is made obsolete by the introduction of another higher-specification model.

With these sorts of fluctuating markets, where the life of a product may not be very long, ongoing product development will be essential, possibly leading to ongoing research and development to retain competitive advantage.

New products into new markets

Diversification with new products into new markets is the riskiest of the four strategies. In many ways this can be likened to starting a business all over again. The research and analysis of your target market will be crucial because you are entering uncharted waters. Because of this diversification must be considered as a long-term strategy, as it may be difficult to reap any rewards in the short term. There are two main forms that diversification can take:

◆ **Related diversification** – the development of new products that are complementary to the existing product range.

◆ **Unrelated diversification** – products that take the business outside of the industry in which it normally operates.

UNDERSTANDING PRODUCT MANAGEMENT

Product management is a critical function for all businesses. It relates to the overall brand image of your product. Getting this right could make or break your business. Brand image can take many forms. It could simply be the name of the business, as in 'Dell Computers'. Alternatively, it could be the name of the product, for example 'Branston Pickle'. Or it could be that it is the overall name for a range of products, such as the 'George' clothing range sold through Asda stores.

It is clear that brand image is closely linked to competitive advantage. It is essential that your brand is easily identified and your choice of name obviously must be very carefully considered. In addition, you must take all available steps to protect the reputation of your brand. It will not matter whether your brand relates to your entire business or a single product – once tarnished it may affect your competitive advantage.

Many businesses, especially new start businesses, do not consider the importance of brand image from the outset. This is a fundamental mistake. All businesses, no matter how large they are now, probably started from very small beginnings. Brand image can only be built up over time, it does not happen overnight.

Setting the Right Price

8

When setting a price the overriding factor to consider is that your objective must be to make a profit. However, that does not necessarily mean that you must make a profit from the outset. One pricing strategy could involve a low initial price purely to quickly gain market share. On the other hand, with a totally new and innovative product, your initial strategy may be to charge as high a price as the market will stand.

You will appreciate, then, that the price will vary to meet the changing demands of the market, by the supply and demand for the product within the market. The major factors affecting pricing decisions are:

◆ customers
◆ costs
◆ competitors
◆ business objectives.

The first of these – customers – is of significant importance. Whilst you have to achieve a price that will gain an eventual profit, you also need a price that will entice consumers to make a purchase.

HOW IMPORTANT IS PRICE TO THE CONSUMER?

To answer this question it is necessary to consider the factors that influence the consumer's decision to make a purchase. Initially, consider the fact that the actual purchaser is not always the same person who made the buying decision, nor are they necessarily the person who will actually use the product.

There are four main groupings that can be used to outline the individuals involved in the purchasing process. They could be represented by up to four different people, or indeed be one and the same person.

- **Users** – the person who will actually use the product. For example, the product may be a gift of some description purchased by someone else.
- **Deciders** – the person who actually takes the decision to make a purchase but who does not necessarily buy the product themselves.
- **Buyers** – The person who actually buys the product. They may not, however, have taken the decision to purchase or be the end user.
- **Influencers** – people who may have some influence over the decision to purchase – children, for example.

Buyer behaviour factors

When considering pricing you need to be aware that consumers can often have some very strange ideas about what constitutes 'the right price'. The purchasing choice can be influenced by perceived risk. In this context, a higher price seems to reduce the risk factor because of greater perceived quality in the product. The most expensive product need not actually offer greater quality.

> **TIP**
>
> As part of your research make sure that you understand the pricing perceptions of the potential customers in your market.

As examples of the deliberations of consumers relating to pricing, consider the following:

- A reduced price can mean that there is something wrong with the product and it may be faulty in some way.
- If quality is established a reduced price could mean a bargain.

◆ A cut in price could be followed in due course by further reductions and so the purchasing decision is delayed.

◆ Numerous changes in price cause confusion.

◆ The true price, especially for products purchased by way of necessity, may not be known by the consumer.

◆ Small price reductions, from say £10.00 to £9.99, are perceived as offering better value.

◆ Large discounts usually make the consumer think that the product could be obsolete in the market.

As you can see, it is sometimes difficult to understand what goes on in the mind of the consumer. You could, for instance, enter the market with a cheaper comparative product than your competition but still fail to gain sales because, rightly or wrongly, your product is considered to be of inferior quality. This is where your market research is critical: understand what the consumer is prepared to pay and what they see as being of higher priority – reduced price or higher quality.

There will never be a right price for all consumers. The influence that consumers have over price cannot be emphasised enough. You ignore the views of the consumer at your peril.

SELECTING THE RIGHT PRICE FOR YOUR PRODUCTS

You will have already gathered that there are a number of important factors to consider when setting the right price for your products. In reality, the price of your product will fall within a defined range. At one end will be the marginal cost of the product, the price below which you cannot afford to sell and still make a profit. At the other end, the price will be the maximum that the market will stand.

TIP

For obvious reasons you should aim to charge the highest price that you can for your products – remember the importance of profitability.

You now need to consider the remaining three factors affecting pricing decisions:

◆ costs
◆ competitors
◆ business objectives.

Costs

You obviously need to cover all costs and have a margin above that in order to make a profit. This will be closely related to the volume of products that you sell and the overhead costs of your business.

Competitors

When selecting your own pricing strategies you will need to consider how your competitors will react. This, in itself, could be defined by the overall market conditions and how strong your competitors are in that market.

Business objectives

The price of your products must reflect your overall business objectives. For example, if you wish to be seen to have a high quality product you will not attempt to undercut your competition with a lower price.

TECHNIQUES FOR FIXING A PRICE

A variety of techniques can be used to fix the price of a product. They can be applied in most business situations whether you are a retailer, a manufacturer, or a service provider.

◆ Cost-plus pricing – a fixed percentage or amount is added to the basic cost of the product.
◆ Break-even pricing – similar to cost-plus pricing, the break-even point of producing a product is established and then an element of profit is added.

◆ Value perception pricing – market research is used to obtain information from the potential consumer as to how much they would be prepared to pay for the product.

◆ Pricing at the going rate – products are priced at a similar cost to those offered by competitors.

USING PRICE AS AN EFFECTIVE MARKETING TOOL

Within your marketing strategy, price can be used in a number of different ways to reflect your overall business objectives and in support of your promotion techniques.

Linking price with promotion

Promotional pricing techniques can be used to achieve short-term gain but with the overall intention of achieving long-term objectives. There are a number of ways in which price can be used to tempt consumers. Consider the following examples:

◆ **Loss leaders** – products sold at low prices that individually make a loss, but entice the consumer into the shop, after which they may well buy other products at the same time. Supermarkets frequently do this, with a range of products being reduced on 'special offer' at any one time.

◆ **Discounts or 'sales'** – these are often used to dispose of excess stock. Just because the price is reduced does not mean that a profit is not still being made. In addition, the higher level of sales could generate more cash than would normally be the case. If working capital is being funded by borrowing, the lower level of debt could reduce interest charges.

◆ **Short-term interest free credit** – this is often used to tempt the consumer to 'buy now and pay later'. Provided the business can fund working capital for the interest-free period this can be a major inducement, especially for larger 'one off' purchases such as a new home heating system. It is also possible that the price can be maintained at a high level, the consumer treating the 'interest free' offer as a discount.

◆ **Maintenance or other service guarantees** – these can either be sold alongside the product or offered on a 'free' basis. On household appliances such as washing machines where, apart from the manufacturer's usual guarantee of perhaps 12 months, an extended warranty might be offered. On motor vehicles, servicing for the first year is usually included in the price but this could be extended as a further inducement. Other 'extras', such as free insurance, may be offered.

> **TIP**
>
> Promotional pricing can be an effective way of quickly gaining a significant share of the market.

Target market pricing

Different prices can often be charged depending on the different market segments or consumer groups that are being targeted.

◆ **Market segment** – if you have segmented your potential market on, for example, a nationwide basis, it is possible to charge different prices according to location. The purchase price of a can of soft drink is substantially different when purchased at a supermarket compared to that at an open air festival.

◆ **Consumer group** – differential pricing depending on the consumer, is a very common pricing structure. The provision of lower prices for students and pensioners is a standard system on the railways where discount cards are available. Most museums, cinemas and theatres offer a discount to both of these groups of consumer.

Opportunist pricing

Sometimes a product can be priced with no relationship to its true value. This could perhaps also be considered as exploitation of the circumstances. Some years ago I was at an open air concert where, against all the weather forecasts, it started to rain quite heavily. One enterprising individual appeared selling black bin liners at £1 each to use as an impromptu 'raincoat'. Needless to say he did quite well. Exploitation, yes, but was I happy to pay? Also yes, it saved me from a soaking.

> **TIP**
>
> Never be afraid to price your products on an opportunist basis, especially if you have a new innovative product with absolutely no competition.

Added value pricing

This involves a different price for products that increasingly offer further features and benefits as in the retail clothes market. A manufacturer may provide essentially the same garment within a range but with increasing quality. For example, an unlined pair of trousers, then a lined pair, then a pair with more pockets. As quality increases, so will the price. This could persuade the consumer to spend slightly more than they originally intended. This can happen more often if the pricing differential between the garments is relatively small in relation to the perceived extra quality.

Linked product pricing

Where one product requires another product as a matter of course, the pricing of both constituent parts can be manipulated. The one product likely to be the required in the long term, could be priced at a substantial discount. The profit to be made will come from the sales of the product with the shortest life. Consider a 'wet shave' razor. It is not the handle that is the most expensive part. The manufacturer makes money on the sale of the razor blades which will, of course, fit only their own handle.

Dual charging

The most common example of this pricing strategy is in the rental industry. In car rentals a basic charge per day is often made with a further charge depending on the mileage driven. The telecommunications industry is another example. A standard monthly or quarterly fee is charged for line rental, a further charge being made for each telephone call.

> **TIP**
>
> Linked product pricing and dual charging can help you with brand loyalty – satisfied customers should bring about repeat business for you.

9
Employing New Staff

As your business expands it is likely that you will need to employ people to work within your business. Quite apart from the statutory responsibilities that you will have as an employer, you will also have to manage your staff to ensure that they are efficient and effective. The first obstacle you will need to overcome is to make sure that you employ the right person for the job.

For the first-time employer, the process of recruitment and selection can be fraught with danger. Employing the wrong person for the job can do significant damage to a small business. You may have already built up a good reputation for your work, all of which can be lost overnight by engaging a new employee without your own high standards.

RECRUITMENT AND SELECTION

As soon as you have identified the need for a new employee you must consider carefully the recruitment and selection process. To gain the right employee for the job you first need to establish a number of factors concerning the job itself. For example:

◆ What exactly will the job entail?
◆ Are any special skills involved?
◆ What type of knowledge will be required?
◆ What sort of personal characteristics will the employee need?
◆ How much supervision will the employee require?
◆ What will be the working conditions, place of work, hours, etc.?
◆ How much will the employee be paid?

Once you have considered all of the factors relating to the job you can then write a formal job description, together with the terms and conditions of employment.

Writing a job description

This is an area where most business owners employing for the first time fall down. The job description that they write is bland and meaningless. Often, all it does is outline what is to be done in the job rather than what the employee is expected to achieve. Consider the following example:

Job Description – Administrative assistant

Duties: Answer the telephone

Deal with incoming faxes

Maintain the office filing system

General typing for the owner

Open the daily mail and deliver outgoing mail to the Post Office

Ask yourself the question – does this really tell the potential employee what I expect of them? Of course it does not! Each of the stated duties is ambiguous, for instance, what does 'deal with incoming faxes' mean? Does it mean take them from the machine and pass them to the owner? Or perhaps it means the employee should formulate and send a response?

You must think through the job description carefully because it will form the basis of the contractual relationship between you and the employee. If you establish from the outset what you want the employee to achieve in working for you there can be no doubts later.

Methods of recruitment

There are a number of methods of recruitment that you can use such as:

◆ newspaper advertisements
◆ careers services
◆ recruitment agencies
◆ The Employment Service and Job Centre.

If you are a first-time employer I would suggest that you use the final option, your local Employment Service. They are likely to have a pool of people that will fit your requirements. In addition, the Employment Service can help you in many other ways. They can assist with:

◆ establishing a suitable job description
◆ defining the terms and conditions of employment
◆ setting the right wage or salary for the job
◆ making a suitable selection
◆ financial incentives to you as the employer.

In the latter case, if you employ someone who is currently unemployed and who meets various criteria, it is likely that some form of financial incentive to employ that person will be available. In general, this will involve a payment to cover part or all of the new employee's wages for a period of six months. In return you will have to provide an agreed training programme to the new member of staff.

TIP

Use the services of the Employment Service from the outset. Their assistance is free and they can help you through the recruitment process.

Making a selection

Once you have a pool of candidates for the new job you then have to decide how to make a selection. Screen all the candidates to ensure that they meet the criteria for the job. You will not wish to waste both your and their time by interviewing all of the prospective candidates. Select a small number that you actually wish to interview.

This is an area in which the Employment Service can help you. They can talk through with you the attributes of all the potential candidates they have to help you decide which ones you would like to see. They can then help you with the actual interview process, as well as your final choice of new employee.

As you are a new employer, the Employment Service can give you guidance on both your responsibilities as an employer and the rights that the employee has. The legislation in this area is extremely complex and you will need all the help that you can get.

YOUR RESPONSIBILITIES AS AN EMPLOYER

Once you employ a member of staff you have a number of statutory responsibilities. First, you must arrange Employers' Liability insurance. This is required to provide protection against your liability for accidental injury or death of an employee whilst at work.

An employee has the right to a written statement setting out the details of their employment. Some of the necessary information should already have been discussed and agreed as part of the recruitment and selection process. For clarity, however, the statement must contain all of the following information:

- The name of the employer and the name of the employee together with their job title and job description.
- Their place of work.
- The date on which the employee commenced work.
- The terms and conditions relating to hours of work and holiday entitlement including public holidays.
- The scale and rate of pay together with payment dates and methods of calculation.
- Procedures in the event of a grievance.
- Sickness procedures including entitlement to sick pay.
- Details of pension schemes.
- Length of notice required to terminate employment.
- Disciplinary rules including the process and any appeal arrangements.

> **TIP**
>
> Whilst the final piece of information is not a statutory requirement for businesses with less than 20 employees, it would be good practice to include it within your statement.

Discrimination

You need to be aware of the legislation covering discrimination and equal opportunities. Jobs, training and promotion must be open to all regardless of colour, race, religion, nationality, ethnic or national origin, sex or marital status.

> **TIP**
>
> Obtain copies of the Dti publications 'Employing Staff' and 'Setting up in Business' reference numbers URN 00/1312 and URN 00/889 respectively.

The discrimination laws apply to all parts of an employee's job including wages and holiday entitlements. You may also have to take into account the provisions of the Disability Discrimination Act. Whilst there are some exemptions for businesses employing less than 15 people, other parts of the Act apply to all businesses.

Health and Safety

You have a responsibility to ensure that, as far as reasonably possible, the health, safety and welfare of your employees is not put at risk whilst they are at work. If you employ five or more employees you must have a written statement of your general health and safety policy and how you carry it out.

You may also need to register your business with either the Health and Safety Executive (HSE) or your Local Authority. The HSE produces a number of publications, some free and others at a modest cost. Contact them for specific advice on how the Health and Safety Acts will affect your business.

THE RIGHTS OF YOUR EMPLOYEE

Legislation covering the rights of your employee is extensive and constantly changing and it would be impossible to explain them in detail. Obtain appropriate advice from the Employment Service before you even take on a new employee. Some of the rights that you will need information on include:

◆ terms and conditions of employment
◆ fair and unfair dismissal
◆ notice periods to terminate employment
◆ membership or non-membership of a Trade Union
◆ redundancy payments
◆ National Minimum Wage
◆ maternity and parental leave
◆ stakeholder pensions
◆ statutory sick pay
◆ statutory maternity pay
◆ working time regulations.

> **TIP**
>
> The Dti publication 'Employing Staff' contains full details of a substantial number of other publications which cover the rights that your employee has.

DEALING WITH TAX AND NATIONAL INSURANCE

For all new employers dealing with the implications of tax and National Insurance deductions fills them with dread. The employee's income tax, subject to a few exemptions in the case of low earnings, together with National Insurance, must be deducted at source under the Pay As You Earn (PAYE) scheme.

As soon as you employ someone you must inform the Inland Revenue. They will automatically send you a comprehensive information pack with all the forms that you will need, including comprehensive tables on how much you should deduct from your employee's wages and where and how you should account for this money to the Inland Revenue.

> **TIP**
>
> The Inland Revenue recognises that employers may have difficulty in filling in all the necessary forms and returns. For this reason they operate various forms of assistance which you can take advantage of.

Many people unfortunately have a negative view of the Inland Revenue as a bureaucratic organisation. The amount of advice and support that the Inland Revenue will give a new employer is, however, limitless and, more importantly, totally free.

Helpline for new employers

If you are thinking of employing for the first there is a special helpline you can telephone:

◆ to register your payroll and PAYE records
◆ to obtain a tailored pack containing all the information, tables and forms that you will require to start your payroll records
◆ to obtain detailed help and guidance on all aspects of running a payroll, including how to fill in the forms and make the returns.

Tailored help and support

The Inland Revenue have a number of business support teams to provide help to all new and small employers. This will cover all aspects of running a payroll including:

◆ what you need to do
◆ the deadlines you must meet
◆ the forms you need to fill in
◆ the records that you need to keep.

This service is offered free and a member of the business support team can come and see you in your place of business, or any other place to suit you. The advisor will talk through any problems you may be encountering and, if you so wish, can check that your payroll system will be adequate to meet their requirements.

Workshops

The Inland Revenue offer a series of half-day workshops specially designed for new and small employers. These cover all aspects of the PAYE scheme including:

Becoming self-employed

This workshop will explain all the records that you need to keep, and outline how to work out your own tax and National Insurance.

Paying your employees

You will learn how to work out your employees' tax and National Insurance contributions, the records that you need to keep and, if required, how you can obtain further assistance.

Paying directors

If you have established your business as a limited company this workshop will explain the special rules for paying directors of the company.

Paying expenses and giving benefits to employees

This covers the most common types of expenses and benefits that are paid to employees and explains the tax and National Insurance implications.

Statutory Sick Pay (SSP) and Statutory Maternity Pay (SMP)

This workshop will explain how to pay SSP and SMP to eligible employees and what to do if an employee is not eligible. It will also explain what you need to do to set up appropriate systems in both cases.

ASSESSING THE PERFORMANCE OF YOUR STAFF

Once you have employed the right person for the job, you must then monitor their performance to ensure that they are effective in their work. Hopefully, you will have set the employee realistic goals and targets from the start of their employment. This, at the very least, will give you some measure of their performance.

Most large businesses will have some form of appraisal system in place for all of their staff. In some cases this will link to promotion prospects and possibly some form of monetary or other performance bonus. For a small business, this type of formal system is not necessary but you still need to have some form of assessment and monitoring process in place. This system could be extremely important if, for example, you consider dismissing an employee for any reason.

There are a number of other reasons why some form of assessment could actually assist your business. It can help with:

◆ **Motivating staff** by giving them praise and perhaps reward for good performance.

◆ **Identifying any development or training requirements** – this can often be delegated to the member of staff to define how and where they wish to extend their knowledge and experience.

◆ **Planning for growth** – it will give you an idea of whether the existing staff can cope with the expansion of the business or whether you will require additional staff.

> **TIP**
>
> Always take time to talk to your staff and encourage them to share any problems – any problems that your staff have mean that your business also has a problem.

The basics of staff assessment

There are a number of basic steps that you need to consider if your assessment process is going to be effective. You need to decide:

◆ what it is exactly that you are going to assess
◆ how often you will carry out an assessment
◆ how you will undertake that assessment
◆ what structure the assessment should take.

What are you going to assess?

If you have targets these will be easy to include as part of the assessment. These targets will also be tangible, i.e. they are easily measured. Intangible components are more difficult to assess. These could include:

◆ communication skills
◆ technical knowledge
◆ standard of customer service
◆ effectiveness at solving problems.

How often will you carry out an assessment?

You should, of course, be making an assessment on an ongoing basis. The point that you have to decide is how often you will communicate that assessment to the employee. You should probably make an assessment after the first three months. After that, you may decide on half-yearly or annual assessments.

How will you make the assessment?

An appropriate scale on which to gauge performance is necessary under appropriate gradings from, say, one to five. These might represent:

1. Unsatisfactory
2. Below standard
3. Satisfactory
4. Good
5. Outstanding.

Structuring the assessment

Having decided on what you are going to assess and the method you are going to employ to go about it, you need to discuss your proposed assessment process with the employee. By doing this you can explain to them what type of behaviour you are looking for, especially in the intangible factors that were looked at earlier. It may be that you can agree simple forms of measurement – for example, all incoming telephone calls to be answered within four rings.

> **TIP**
>
> If the employee does not understand why and how they are being assessed this could lead to a lack of motivation and feelings of resentment.

It is important to allocate sufficient, uninterrupted time for your discussions. The process does not have to be undertaken on a formal interview basis. In some cases, it is better to have an informal approach so that the employee does not feel threatened by the assessment.

They need reassurance that it is a two-way process. You are trying to help them improve and, if they have their own ideas as to how they can improve, perhaps by accepting more responsibility, it is their opportunity to discuss this with you.

10 Being in the Right Place

Place considerations do not relate solely to physical location. They also relate to how and when your products will be offered, in short, the distribution management techniques that you will use to solve three key issues:

◆ being in the right place
◆ at the right time
◆ with the right amount of products.

The distribution techniques that you use will depend on your type of business. Different considerations will apply depending on whether you are a service business, a retailer, a wholesaler or a manufacturer. In all cases, you will need to concentrate on the demands of the consumer and the characteristics of the market.

As with all aspects of marketing you must not forget the importance of competitive advantage. New and innovative distribution techniques may enable you to reach markets and consumers that were previously unavailable. The increasing use of the Internet, for example, has opened up new opportunities for small businesses to compete with large multinational companies on a global basis.

UNDERSTANDING THE IMPORTANCE OF LOCATION

The importance to your business of physical location will depend on the type of business that you operate. For a retailer, for example, it may be extremely important to be in a location with a high volume of passing trade, while a mobile car mechanic need have no physical location, apart from their vehicle. In this case, the question of location will only be relevant in terms of the geographical area in which they operate.

To explore the importance of place decisions further, let us consider the implications for the four main types of business:

- retailers
- wholesalers
- manufacturers
- service businesses.

Retailers

Having the right shop location is undoubtedly an important factor in this sector of business, provided you intend to operate on a face-to-face basis with your customers. As extreme examples, take the following cases and decide which would receive the most sales:

- a book retailer in a popular shopping mall
- a book retailer in an industrial unit on a trading estate.

You have probably chosen the shop in the shopping mall. But are you right? Have you considered how they are distributing their books? The first shop is obviously dealing direct with the public on a face-to-face basis. That does not mean, however, that they are making more sales. What if the book shop on the trading estate only deals with the public through mail order?

You can see from this example that decisions on location do not relate to just one aspect, but to a combination of factors which will depend on how you intend to deal with your customers. Because of the Internet, in some cases it is no longer necessary to have a physical location for the customer to visit.

TIP
Take extreme care when you select the location for your shop – you must ensure that there is no immediate competitor in the same locality.

This aspect will have the greatest impact on a retailer. Even if you operate one small shop, you should probably have a presence on the Internet through which you can sell. More and more shopping will be undertaken from home and you need to consider the Internet as part of your place decision.

Wholesalers

To a wholesaler the consideration of place will not be of prime importance. Provided they are within a reasonable distance of the retailing outlets who will provide most of their business, and there is adequate car parking, physical location will not be a major factor.

What will be important, however, will be the ease with which deliveries can be accepted from manufacturers. It would be blatantly unwise to establish a wholesaling business without access to adequate roads being in place to accommodate the large delivery wagons. It will also be necessary to ensure that appropriate equipment – for example, fork lift trucks – can operate effectively within the wholesale premises.

All of these factors may not immediately come to mind but they will play a part in the success of your business. You will need to consider also the physical layout of the interior of your premises. Your customers need to have easy access to all of your goods and, perhaps more importantly to them, easy means by which to transport them from your premises to their own vehicles.

Manufacturers

Physical location may or may not play a role in your consideration of place. It will, to some extent, depend on what you are manufacturing. It will also partly depend on the supply of components, if any, that you need to manufacture your finished product.

As examples, consider the aircraft and railway industries. The aircraft manufacturer will require an extensive physical location complete with airport runway facilities. The railway carriage manufacturer will probably require, at the very least, easy access to railway lines to deliver the completed product.

A manufacturer of a high technology product, say computer chips, may be more concerned about the interior of their premises than their geographical location. It will be more important for them to have a 'sterile' interior in order to avoid product contamination.

The manufacture of a product that relies on components from other manufacturers ideally requires a location close to those suppliers. The motor manufacturer Nissan decided to locate in the North East of England due to the proximity of good quality component manufacturers that were already established in the same area. This was, of course, in addition to the local and central government incentives that were made available to them.

> **TIP**
>
> Make sure your factory space is more than adequate for your immediate requirements – allow room for modest expansion over the next few years.

Service businesses

The question of physical location will be relatively unimportant to businesses in the service sector. Nevertheless, there are service businesses where location can play a role. Take Harley Street in London as an example, an internationally recognised location for the medical profession.

In the same way, the legal profession seems to be consistently grouped together in the same location within a town. Whether this helps or hinders their individual practice is open to question. It is difficult to see a competitive advantage being offered in such circumstances.

For most service businesses, the most important aspect of location will be the geographical area in which they operate. In the example above, consider the mobile car mechanic who may decide only to operate within a strictly defined area. This could be for a number of reasons. It could be that there are no local competitors, or that the additional costs in terms of time and money would make longer journeys relatively unprofitable.

ESTABLISHING THE METHODS OF DISTRIBUTION

Here also, the methods of distribution will depend upon the sector of business in which you operate. There may, in effect, be a number of tiers through which your products progress on their way to the consumer. Consider the following flow diagram:

Manufacturer ⟶ Wholesaler ⟶ Retailer ⟶ Consumer

The number of people who handle your products will depend on where you are sited within the chain. On the other hand, the chain for a service business will be direct, i.e.:

Service ⟶ Consumer

When considering your distribution strategies you have three basic choices:

◆ selective distribution
◆ exclusive distribution
◆ intensive distribution.

Selective distribution

With this method you would be highly selective about how you distribute your products. The way in which you sell your product could be defined by the perception of the consumer. For example, a consumer would not expect to purchase a computer system from a garage forecourt.

Exclusive distribution

Normally associated with products perceived to be of high or unique quality, exclusive distribution would limit availability of your products. This might seem a restrictive strategy but it is used to enhance the perception of exclusivity to the consumer.

Intensive distribution

As the name would suggest, this strategy aims to make your products as widely available as possible. The number of outlets will be substantial but this will only work where there is also intensive demand.

> **TIP**
>
> Try to keep your distribution as simple as possible – the longer the chain the more the price will increase to the customer.

DESIGNING THE RIGHT DISTRIBUTION SYSTEM

There are a number of factors that you need to bear in mind when designing your distribution system. First we will concentrate on the distribution of your products to the consumer.

The key to a successful distribution system is co-ordination. As we have seen, the links in the distribution process all need to be successfully managed. It does not matter where you are in the process, you still need to ensure that your products are available in the right place at the right time to enable them to be purchased.

In relation to distribution, your customers will want to be sure about a number of factors, most of which can be covered under three headings:

◆ reliability
◆ suitability
◆ functionality.

Reliability

Your customers will want to be sure that you can be relied on to deliver the right products at the right time. Advertising products that are out of stock or delivered late will not help your marketing image.

Suitability

Having recieved or bought your product, the customer will need to be sure that it is suitable for its intended purpose. It is therefore vitally important that your products are packaged in such a way that they will not be damaged in the distribution process. Whilst this may mainly apply to a manufacturer, it is also an important consideration for both wholesalers and retailers.

Functionality

Having bought the product and found it to be suitable, the consumer will also be concerned about what happens if it fails to function in the future. If the product breaks down through no fault of the consumer, quite apart from their statutory rights, they will expect the product to be repaired or replaced. This may, or may not, be covered by any service guarantees that you offer.

MANAGING THE SUPPLY CHAIN EFFECTIVELY

Your customers expect your products to be in the right place at the right time and in sufficient quantity. As a customer yourself you also have the same expectation from your suppliers. It is not the reputation of your supplier that will be tarnished if you are unable to provide your customer with a product. It will be your reputation that suffers.

This aspect is often overlooked in the concept of marketing. It is, however, vitally important. For some goods there is an acceptance by the consumer that they may have to wait for final delivery, as with mail order. Another example would be goods that are specially ordered, such as a bespoke suit.

In both cases, co-ordination will again play an important part. Many mail order businesses carry little or no stocks of the products they offer. They rely on specialist distribution suppliers or warehouses. Quite simply, it is often the case that they cannot afford to carry sufficient stocks with the inevitable costs that are involved. For this reason you will often see the following, or something similar, on their order forms: 'Please allow 28 days for delivery'.

> **TIP**
>
> Once you have given a specific delivery date make sure that you do deliver on time.

It is obviously important that your supplier is able actually to supply the product either to you, or direct to the consumer. If the consumer has ordered goods from you, they have accepted the defined delay in delivery. If, however, this accepted delay is exceeded, once again your reputation could be tarnished as you are thought unreliable. This is despite the fact that it is your supplier who has caused the problem.

As part of your distribution strategy you therefore need to consider the question of appropriate suppliers for your business. Unless you only have one source of supply you need to have details of alternative suppliers that could be used at short notice. Better still would be to use a number of suppliers at any one time. This may impact on any volume discounts that are made available to you but, if the quality is the same, this could be a small price to pay for reliability.

11 Promoting Your Business

Many businesses make the mistake of considering only their advertising material as promotion. Promotion is more than this. Promotion is all about the way in which you communicate with your customers. In plain terms, it is saying the right thing to the right people. This means that everything that you do, from your stationery and business cards through to the format and presentation of your advertisements, must convey the right message.

The mix of communication strategies that you can use for promotion is virtually endless. The important part is selecting those that will provide you with the most return. Always remember that the most expensive option is not always the best option. Reputation and image also play a large part and these cannot be bought; they have to be earned.

UNDERSTANDING THE IMPORTANCE OF PROMOTION

TIP

Always carry a supply of business cards even when you go out socially – the conversation may turn to what you do for a living and you may gain a potential customer.

Unless potential customers know about you and your products it will be difficult for you to make any sales. You may have the finest, most innovative product in the world, but unless you communicate how and where it can be bought, and at what price, nobody will even be aware of its existence.

Promotion strategies, or perhaps to give them more direct meaning, communication strategies, are therefore vital to your business. In order to communicate successfully with your potential customers you need to understand:

◆ who they are
◆ what they are looking to purchase
◆ what makes them decide to buy a particular product
◆ how much they are prepared to pay
◆ where they expect to buy from.

You must also have clear promotion objectives before you can begin to consider strategy. It is not sufficient to concentrate your promotion methods purely on sales objectives. The question of linking your objectives to your promotion strategy is important and is looked at later in this chapter. For the moment, though, you should understand the five essential components of promotion strategy:

◆ Potential customers must be made aware of your existence.
◆ They need to know what products you are offering.
◆ They must be advised how your products will satisfy their needs.
◆ They must perceive your product as being the best to suit their needs.
◆ They must then be persuaded actually to make a purchase.

As with all forms of communication there are at least two interested parties – the sender of the message and the recipient. In order to make the communication meaningful it must also have four essential components:

◆ who it is to be sent to
◆ what it will say
◆ how it will be sent
◆ the desired effect.

The first of these should have been covered in your market research where you identified your target market. The last one is, of course, the desire that potential customers will make a purchase. The middle two, however, require extensive thought. If you send the wrong message you could alienate your target audience. The message also needs to be sent by the most appropriate medium. There is little point, for example, in advertising your golf products in a gardening magazine.

One of the most important aspects of your promotion strategy will be the unique selling points that were looked at in Chapter 6. These will form part of your competitive advantage and, as such, should be clearly communicated in all of your promotional activities.

THE MARKETING PROMOTION MIX

There is no perfect mix of promotion techniques that will be suitable for all businesses. What you do need to do is use a number of different techniques and keep statistics to enable you to evaluate those that are working and those that are not.

A good business will always keep pace with changes in communication techniques, trying out new or different ones, and monitoring the effect on sales. Unless you know how you are gaining business it will be difficult to concentrate your efforts on those that are profitable and avoid those that are not.

The marketing communication mix is comprised essentially of four different types of promotion techniques:

◆ advertising
◆ public relations and publicity
◆ sales promotions
◆ personal selling.

With the increasing use of the Internet for promotion and sales purposes, a new dimension is now added. For any business looking to keep pace with technological advancements it must be separately incorporated into your promotion techniques.

Advertising

Advertising in one form or another is probably the most common form of promotion for all businesses. It can be done in a number of different ways using a wide variety of mediums. These could include:

> **TIP**
>
> Before you advertise in a particular magazine or newspaper make sure that you look at a copy to ensure that your advert will not be out of place.

◆ television or radio
◆ posters
◆ press.

Quite apart from all these forms of advertising you must remember that everything about your business must be used to communicate with potential customers. As part of your communication mix relating to advertising you can also use:

◆ standard styles and logos on all your business stationery
◆ leaflets and brochures that conform to the standard style
◆ appropriate sign-writing on all your vehicles.

Whatever form your advertising takes, you need to take great care to select the right medium. Advertising is not necessarily of significant use for all businesses. When looking at advertising you will need to consider the potential market and the location of potential customers. This is examined in greater detail a little later in this chapter.

Public relations and publicity

Many businesses totally ignore this important component of the communication mix. You have only to read the business pages of any newspaper to see the results of a successful public relations exercise. Always remember, the business editor starts out with a blank page. If you can provide newsworthy items to help them fill the page they will be very grateful.

Do not underestimate the power of such free editorial coverage. In real terms, it can do more for your business than a paid advertisement. It tells potential customers what you are doing and, more importantly, brings you to their attention.

If you have any news that could be used to promote your business in the eyes of your potential consumers then always prepare a press release. Even if you only send it to a few select local newspapers the only cost to you is your time in preparing the content.

> **TIP**
>
> You have nothing to lose in telephoning the business editor of your local paper if you have something newsworthy – even if they do not have space for the item now they may use you as a feature in the future.

Sales promotions

Sales promotions come in a wide variety of forms, not all of which are directed at the consumer. In broad terms, sales promotion techniques can be categorised into three headings:

◆ trade
◆ consumer
◆ internal.

Trade

If you are a manufacturer, you can offer incentives to wholesalers or retailers to sell your products. These could take the form of either financial or non-financial incentives. Financial incentives could include discounts or extended credit terms. Non-financial incentives may be the provision of free display materials.

Consumer

These are incentives directed at the consumer either at the point of sale or through advertisements. They could include 'money off' vouchers or coupons. Free samples of the product or demonstrations may also be made available.

Internal

Incentives of one form or another may be offered to your sales staff. These might include bonuses or other financial awards for meeting, or exceeding, sales targets. Great care, however, is required with this form of inducement to ensure that it complies with current Inland Revenue guidelines.

> **TIP**
>
> If you are going to use telesales as one of your promotion techniques then you must seek advice – there are strict guidelines that must be followed.

Personal selling

As the name would suggest, this is sales promotion direct to the consumer using personal contact. This can be either face to face or over the telephone. It can also be achieved utilising trade fairs or exhibitions, for example, the Ideal Home Exhibition.

Using the Internet

Sales over the Internet are predicted to rise substantially over the coming years. This brings a new dimension to the concept of home shopping.

Quite apart from this aspect, there is no reason why your business cannot use computers to aid you in other areas of business planning.

It is not necessary for you to spend vast sums of money on a website. Indeed, some of the most successful sites are very basic. If you design your website pages full of graphics that take a long time to download you are, in fact, more likely to put off potential customers.

You cannot afford to ignore the opportunities that the Internet will bring for all businesses. It is a vital, and indeed separate, part of your marketing communication mix.

EVALUATING YOUR PROMOTION OPTIONS

Evaluating promotion options is not an easy task. All of the many options have their own advantages and disadvantages. Some options will suit some businesses more than others. For example, a television advertising campaign is unlikely to even be considered by a small business.

Of the four promotion techniques, advertising is by far the hardest to evaluate. For this reason we will concentrate on this one aspect of promotion. The evaluation techniques that you use are, however, just as valid for all the other tools for promotion.

The principle factor that you need to consider when evaluating how and where to advertise is your potential customer:

◆ Who are they?
◆ Where are they?
◆ How can they best be reached?

At this stage you should have the answers to the first two questions. It is the last question that needs to be considered in some depth. In order to do that you are going to have to answer some pertinent questions:

What exactly are you selling?

Whether you advertise at all will depend on your product. Some products, especially those in large markets, will require extensive advertising campaigns if volume sales are to be achieved. Other products, which perhaps are sold in a highly specialised field, for example hospital equipment, are unlikely to be sold through advertising. Other forms of promotion, such as participation in trade exhibitions, might be used.

What are the market conditions?

Market conditions will play a large part in your decision on whether to advertise or not. If all of your competitors advertise then it is likely that you will decide to do so as well, though not necessarily in the same way or in the same publications. In some markets, advertising is unnecessary or even prohibited. The medical profession is a prime example of the latter.

> **TIP**
>
> Make sure that your advertising is appropriate to the market conditions.

What are your marketing objectives?

You need to be clear on whether advertising fits in with your objectives, and on what it is you hope to achieve. It all comes back to the message you want to send to your potential customer. Even if you are not advertising any particular product at any given moment in time, you may need to advertise just to maintain your brand image. This form of advertising can include sponsorship deals, such as motor racing. Businesses with no connection to the sport pay substantial amounts of money for just a small advert on the racing car to keep their name in front of the consumer.

Is the advertising going to be cost effective?

This is the most important question. Advertising should only be undertaken when it is cost effective. As you will appreciate, it is also extremely difficult, at least initially, to make an assessment of how cost effective it will be. It is therefore crucial that you maintain appropriate statistics on those advertisements that have prompted customers to make a purchase.

Examples of how this is done are given in the press every day. More often than not, if you respond to an advertisement you are asked to quote a reference, which will tell the business where you saw the advertisement. They can then identify where business is coming from, and more importantly, can also tell which of their advertisements are not generating sales.

> **TIP**
>
> Sponsorship can be cost effective in more ways than one. Supplying the football kit for your local team will also generate a lot of goodwill in your local community – just make sure your business name is on the shirt!

USING PROMOTION METHODS TO ACHIEVE OBJECTIVES

So far in this chapter we have looked at the promotion options available to you and how to evaluate them. The time has now come to consider your promotion strategies. In order to do that you must have clear promotion objectives.

The number of promotion objectives that you have can be many and varied. Remember, however, the SMART criteria that we looked at in Chapter 3. The more precise your promotion objectives are, the easier they will be to measure. This aspect is extremely important if you are to avoid wasting money on promotion techniques that do not achieve sales.

You will also need to link your promotional activity to your product portfolio and life cycle analysis that was considered in Chapter 7. In addition, you may need to consider the pricing strategies outlined in Chapter 8.

All of these aspects can impact on your promotion objectives and will, in turn, affect the promotion techniques that you decide to employ. Examples of some promotion objectives you might decide on are:

◆ to introduce a new product to potential customers
◆ to introduce a new product to existing customers
◆ to highlight new features and benefits of an existing product
◆ to bring attention to discounts or special offers
◆ to increase awareness in the market of increased product quality
◆ to retain and build upon brand image
◆ to stimulate repeat business.

Once you have clearly defined your promotion objectives you can start to put together your promotion strategies. If, for example, you were seeking to increase market share with new customers, you would not target existing customers as part of your strategy. On the other hand, if you have developed a new product that would probably be purchased by existing customers as well, your target audience will be both existing and new customers. The whole point is focus.

The promotion strategies that you use must focus on the market and on the customer to whom you are trying to sell. If you attempt to sell a product to the wrong customer, or in the wrong market, it will not matter how good your promotion techniques are, they will fall on deaf ears.

TIP

Whatever promotion techniques you decide to use, make sure that you give them time to work. Advertising does not always work overnight.

Using Professional Help

In starting your business you are going to need all the help you can get. Chapter 5 described the business support that is available. In this chapter we will concentrate on the help that you can obtain from professionals. There are three main categories of professional:

◆ accountants
◆ solicitors
◆ consultants.

Before we look at these individually, a few general words of advice are appropriate. When dealing with any professional, always check their credentials. You need to be aware that there are bogus operators in each and every field of life and you will not want to part with any money for advice that may not be factually correct.

Before you appoint any professional, make sure that you visit their own office. Take time to look around. Does it appear well organised and tidy? Does the telephone ring regularly? Are there general signs of activity? Whilst this sort of personal observation may not apply to consultants who work entirely from a home office, you should also check for relevant professional qualifications or accreditation from a recognised body.

Accountants, for example, should be members of one of the three main professional accounting bodies:

◆ The Institute of Chartered Accountants (ACA)
◆ The Association of Chartered Certified Accountants (ACCA)
◆ The Chartered Institute of Management Accountants (CIMA).

Accreditation should be from a recognised body which only proffers it after stringent criteria have been met. For example, as a consultant I am accredited by the British Accreditation Bureau as a Certified Practitioner to work with businesses in the areas of strategic planning, fund raising and marketing. This accreditation was only gained after I had provided:

◆ three examples of work that had been completed
◆ three references from clients satisfied with my work
◆ proof of professional indemnity insurance
◆ proof of an ongoing programme for continuous professional development.

In addition, I was subjected to a rigorous selection interview during which I had to give a presentation regarding my work as a consultant, outline in detail one of the consultancy projects that I had undertaken and provide documentary evidence of my professional and other qualifications with copies of the relevant certificates.

> **TIP**
>
> If someone claims to be a member of a professional body, do not be afraid to telephone that body to check their standing and credentials.

This accreditation is also subject to annual renewal, with at least three references being necessary from clients for whom I have undertaken work in the preceding 12 months.

CHOOSING AND USING AN ACCOUNTANT

A word of caution to start with. Anyone can call themselves an 'accountant' or a 'book-keeper' despite the fact that they may hold no professional qualifications whatsoever. For obvious reasons, the quality of service that they provide, and the business help and advice that they offer, can vary widely.

All qualified members of the organisations previously referred to in this chapter will have undertaken rigorous examinations before being allowed to use the respective designatory letters of ACA, ACCA, or CIMA. In addition, they are all required to adhere to high professional standards and all of these organisations have established complaint and disciplinary procedures.

All members of these organisations who prepare or audit accounts are required to have a practising certificate. These are renewable annually provided the accountant complies with the requirements relating to professional indemnity insurance, continuing professional development, and the continuity of the practice arrangements outlined by each organisation.

How should you choose an accountant?

The choice of an accountant is very important because they will probably be your primary professional business advisor. You should see them as being a partner, there to assist you with the running of your business. For this reason, the accountant you choose needs to be the right one for you from the very start. This means too that you need to like them on a personal level. They could be the best accountant going but unless you actually like them you are unlikely to be willing to accept their advice regardless of how good it is.

Choosing an accountant also involves the question of their fee. It would be inappropriate for a small business with limited turnover to seek to appoint an accountant from one of the major accountancy practices. The accountant you choose should be the one that is also being used by other businesses the same size as yours, although they will need to be able to cope with your business as it grows.

TIP

If possible, obtain a recommendation from your local Business Link or bank manager for a suitable accountant – they should be able to advise on one that will suit your type and size of business.

The question of what sort of fee is appropriate is difficult and subjective. It depends on what you expect your accountant to do for you. Only you are in a position to assess accurately whether the proposed fee represents value for money. There is nothing to stop you from obtaining comparative quotations. As in any other market, there is plenty of choice.

What can an accountant do for you?

An accountant can help you in a number of different ways including:

◆ complying with legislation
◆ establishing internal control systems
◆ assisting with pricing and profitability decisions
◆ raising finance
◆ managing the growth of your business.

This is not an exhaustive list but is intended to provide you with an idea of the types of services that can be provided. You will note that I have quite purposely omitted the one service you may have expected – preparing accounts.

As the business owner the preparation of accounts is your responsibility. Legislation requires that proper accounting records be kept and it is you, not your accountant, who will pay the penalty if this is not complied with. If you do not have the necessary skills, or perhaps the time, to keep the accounts, then you probably need to delegate this task to a book-keeper.

A book-keeper will not have the specialist skills of an accountant but should be able to maintain your financial records using the double-entry method. They should also be able to produce a trial balance that can then be used by your accountant to prepare the necessary summary financial statements.

What should you expect from your accountant?

As you will have noted earlier, accountants offer a wide range of services and it is really for you to decide what you want them to do. Most accountants are happy to quote for a 'package' of services covering the basic completion of your accounts through to dealing with VAT and other tax returns.

You need to decide what financial accounting you can undertake in-house and weigh this against the costs of using the accountant. It is obviously going to be more cost effective for you to undertake the mundane book-keeping tasks in-house, only calling upon the expertise of your accountant when necessary.

> **TIP**
>
> Try to make your accountant's job easier by keeping records that are in a format that they can easily interpret – you will save money in the long run in terms of the time that they spend looking after your business affairs.

Once your accountant is appointed, they should issue you with a letter of engagement. This should set out quite clearly the tasks that they will perform for you and the fee involved. Finally, do not consider that the fee quoted is cast in stone. As with all service-based businesses, the fee is negotiable depending on the work required.

USING THE SERVICES OF A SOLICITOR

Solicitors provide a range of legal services to businesses. You may already have a solicitor whom you use for personal affairs, but bear in mind that the same solicitor may not be appropriate for your business. If they are not experienced in offering business advice they should be able to provide a recommendation for another solicitor that can help you.

There are a number of areas where a solicitor can help your business. For example:

TIP

Before you consult a solicitor, if you are a member of a Trade Association, for example the Federation of Small Businesses, you may be able to obtain free advice from their own legal specialists.

◆ Deciding on the correct form for your business i.e. sole trader, partnership or limited company.
◆ Checking the terms of the lease for any premises that you are considering taking on.
◆ Advice and guidance on any contractual terms of trade that you are drawing up for your own business or that you are being asked to sign.
◆ Help with the collection of any bad debts – a solicitor's letter often prompts payment!

How much will a solicitor cost?

This will vary depending on the size and location of the practice that you are using. The senior partner of a leading city law firm will cost more than a solicitor in a small town practice. Ideally, as a new business you should choose a smaller firm of solicitors who will value your business and provide a greater standard of personal service.

In terms of the actual fees that you are charged, most solicitors' invoices will have two clear sections:

◆ Details of the work carried out on your behalf with a breakdown of the appropriate hours and amounts involved.
◆ Any costs that the solicitor has incurred on your behalf, for example Companies House registration fees, that are to be passed on to you for payment.

The Law Society requires solicitors to give you information on the likely cost of their work. If you do not receive this you should either ask them for an estimate or alternatively agree a fixed fee at the outset. It is possible that if the matter involves a substantial amount of work

TIP

If there is any part of your solicitor's invoice that you do not understand, seek clarification before you make payment.

you may be asked for a deposit or 'retainer'. Depending upon the circumstances, you will have to decide whether this is reasonable or not.

USING A CONSULTANT

Businesses usually employ a consultant to identify problems within a business and recommend changes that will either solve a problem or improve performance. In some cases, the services of a consultant may be retained to implement effectively the changes recommended.

Consultants are used because they have specialist skills and are able to provide objective and impartial advice, particularly where radical changes need to be implemented which could prove to be a source of conflict within the business.

Consultants are also able to advise on future projects while in the planning stages and increasingly consultants are used as facilitators to advise management and staff who are working through new processes.

Management consultants come from a wide range of backgrounds, although popular qualifications within the industry include accountancy, engineering, marketing, personnel, computing or social sciences. There are also a number of related qualifications which may be useful including a Diploma in Management Studies, a standard Degree in Business Administration or a Masters Degree in Business Administration.

Types of consultancy

Management consultancy practices are involved in the following areas of work:

◆ strategy

◆ organisation design and development

◆ quality management

◆ manufacturing systems

◆ business planning

◆ financial management

◆ project management

◆ information technology/information systems

◆ human resource management

◆ marketing

◆ design and creativity

◆ transport management.

Within these types of consultancy there are also different methods of consulting. Each of the following three methods is distinct and, provided they are appropriate for the circumstances, are all equally valid:

Expertise consulting

This method is often described as a 'surgical approach'. It is an operation that provides an immediate solution to a defined problem, although in the long term the solution may not be a permanent cure.

You will usually define the problem and then hire the consultant to fix it. You may decide that you require a full upgrade to your existing computer system. You would then hire an IT consultant to advise on the appropriate system and software requirement which they may then help to install.

It is possible that they may then run a training course on the use of the new system for your employees. Once this is completed they are unlikely to have any further involvement with your business. It is only to be hoped that the employees take in and understand the training offered and are then able to put it to good use within the business.

Process consulting

As opposed to the expertise method of consulting, process consulting takes more of a 'therapy' approach. It transfers the skills of the consultant to the client to enable them to solve their own problems.

The consultant acts as a sounding board to talk through ideas and perhaps different ways of running the business. Interaction between the parties enables the client to become more confident in running their business.

> **TIP**
>
> This is perhaps the best form of consultant to employ because you will gain added expertise in the running of your business.

Contingency consulting

The final method of consulting is alien to some consultants and businesses because it effectively requires the services of the consultant to be made redundant as soon as possible. Using the surgery and therapy examples, contingency consulting can be likened to a short course of medicine.

It effectively involves the consultant as a facilitator, taking the issues within the problem and redefining them to create a solution. In many cases you will find that you have solved the problem yourself purely by using the consultant to ask the right questions.

Reasons for using a consultant

Consultants are used by businesses for a variety of different reasons. In some cases it may seem strange that the services of a consultant are required when the business apparently already has internal experts that could solve the problem. It would be impossible to try to define all of the reasons for using a consultant, but consider the following examples:

◆ The expertise may be available within the business but the individuals may be unavailable to carry out the task.
◆ The expertise may be unavailable within the business and therefore has to be bought in.
◆ Even if the expertise is available in-house it may be recognised that an outside view can bring a new perspective to solving the problem.
◆ In some cases internal business politics may mean that an outside view is likely to be received more favourably than an internal solution.
◆ A consultant can always be blamed if the solution is unpalatable, or if it goes wrong, which in both cases means that existing social bonds within the business will be kept intact.
◆ In extreme cases an outside body, for example a bank, may insist that the business is reviewed by a consultant on an impartial basis.

TIP

The services of a consultant will not be cheap but they can be extremely cost effective – new opportunities or cost savings for your business could be identified by a consultant who is both independent and unbiased.

13 Compiling Financial Forecasts

Forecast accounts, in cash flow, profit and loss and balance sheet format, are essential to plan your business finances. All too often, however, business owners only prepare them when absolutely necessary and usually for the wrong reasons, possibly at the insistence of your bank. This usually means that you are looking to borrow money, and, if you had prepared them from the outset, you would have seen the need to borrow such money well in advance.

Not having prepared them in advance now places you at a distinct disadvantage. It is more than likely that you have run out of cash and the only way that you can survive is to borrow money. Control of your business has therefore been lost and you are relying on a funder to support you. If you had applied to the funder well in advance, before you actually needed the money, you would have given yourself more options in the event that they should turn your request down.

TIP

Cash is like the flow of blood through your veins. If the flow stops you will die. In the same way, if the flow of cash into your business ceases, your business will not survive.

The only way that you can assess your future finances is by short-term and long-term financial planning. This will cover not just cash, which is of primary importance, but also profitability and growth.

All of the forecasts must be prepared on a realistic basis, and if anything, you must be pessimistic rather than optimistic. This will, in effect, give you the worst case scenario. It is far better to work on this basis and then demonstrate that you can achieve a better performance.

THE CASH FLOW FORECAST

This is probably the most important of all your forecasts. A cash flow forecast is used to project the flow of cash into, and out of, your business. It is not concerned with profitability or growth, it is totally focused on your cash situation, normally referred to as 'liquidity'.

Liquidity, in terms of actual cash, is essential to all businesses no matter what their size. Orders from customers are of no value whatsoever if you do not have the funds to manufacture the goods. In the same way, a warehouse full of stock will not pay the wages unless the goods can be sold and thereby converted into cash.

In simplistic terms cash flows through your business as follows:

From this simple diagram you can see that if any part of the process is disrupted, for example, by late or non-payment by your customers, then you are likely to encounter a shortage of cash. Planning for such disruptions in cash flow will give you greater control over your financial stability and, in the long run, the whole viability of your business.

> **TIP**
>
> You must maintain tight control over your cash position – do not allow your debtors to take advantage of you; they could cause your business to fail.

Income from sales

It is extremely important that you accurately estimate the income that you are going to receive. This forms the whole foundation of your business and if you over-estimate the cash you are going to receive you could be placed in serious difficulty. This has been shown to great effect with the forecasts prepared for the Millennium Dome. So optimistic were the forecasts that within months of opening, with the anticipated visitor numbers not materialising, extra funds had to be obtained to avoid early closure.

Sales income will generally be received either in cash for immediate payment or on credit for payment at a later date. With forecasts, the cash element can be shown as being received in the month the sales were made. The credit sales will be dealt with differently.

Dealing with credit sales

At the outset you will have agreed a defined payment period for your debtors to pay for the sales that you have allowed on credit. This could be for any term from, say, 30 days up to 90 days depending on the industry in which you operate.

Once again, however, you need to be pessimistic with your forecasts. Inevitably there will be some slippage in payment receipts and it is better to build them into your forecasts from the outset. In addition, there could be a small element that abuse the credit facility and take much longer than the standard payment time.

It is normal, therefore, to build a further contingency into your forecasts. If, for example, you offer credit terms of 30 days, some forecasts may be prepared on the basis of 70% of sales being received in the month after the sales have been made. A further 20%

TIP

If your debtors are not paying you on time then do not allow them further credit until they have settled their debt.

of the month one sales will be received in month three with the balance of 10% being received in month four. With experience you will be able to define when payments are actually received.

Other income

Any other income that you receive which is not related to trading activity will be defined separately in the cash flow forecast. Examples include:

◆ introduction of new capital
◆ loans or grants received
◆ receipts from the sale of fixed assets.

Payment categories

The expenditure that you will incur in business will be broken down into a number of different headings. For example:

◆ payments to creditors
◆ salaries and wages
◆ capital expenditure
◆ light, heat and power
◆ rent and rates
◆ loan repayments.

It does not really matter how many different payment categories you have, the important point being that you remain consistent with your headings. This will make it a lot easier to monitor your expenditure and give you the ability later on to compare your forecasted figures with the actual expenditure.

Sample cash flow forecast

Most of the high street banks will have fairly standard cash flow forecast forms and these will help you with the general layout.

In the cash flow forecast on page 130, the following assumptions have been made:

◆ Sales receipts – 50% in cash
    25% after 30 days
    25% after 60 days.
◆ Bank loan of £30,000 is repayable over 10 years with interest fixed at 7.5%.
◆ Grants will be received equating to 5% of capital expenditure.
◆ Raw material costs will equate to 35% of the selling price.
◆ Being a new business no trade credit is available for the first year.
◆ VAT is calculated at 17.5%.

THE PROFIT AND LOSS FORECAST

Once you have completed your cash flow forecasts you can then go on and construct a forecasted profit and loss account. In many ways, it will take the same format as your cash flow forecast, and again most of the high street banks can provide you with standard forms to set out your forecasted profit and loss account. These are generally referred to as 'operating budgets'.

The operating budget

What you need to remember is that this is a forecast, and as such, will need to be compiled with monthly figures. It will not be a summary of your trading position. You must also remember that you are dealing now with profitability and not cash. This will mean that the sales that you make are entered in the actual month in which they occur.

SAMPLE CASH FLOW FORECAST

	1	2	3	4	5	6	7	8	9	10	11	12	TOTAL
SALES													
Product 1	4,000	5,500	6,500	7,500	7,500	7,500	8,500	8,500	8,000	8,000	6,500	6,500	84,500
Product 2	2,000	3,500	5,500	5,500	6,500	6,500	7,000	7,000	7,000	6,500	6,500	6,000	69,500
Product 3	2,000	3,500	5,000	5,000	5,000	8,000	8,000	8,000	5,000	5,000	5,000	5,000	64,500
TOTAL	8,000	12,500	17,000	18,000	19,000	22,000	23,500	23,500	20,000	19,500	18,000	17,500	218,500
RECEIPTS													
Debtors	4,000	8,250	13,625	16,375	18,250	20,250	22,000	23,125	21,750	20,625	18,875	18,125	205,250
Owners	40,000												40,000
Grants	2,000			250			250			250			2,750
Loans	30,000												30,000
Other													0
VAT	700	1,444	2,384	2,866	3,194	3,544	3,850	4,047	3,806	3,609	3,303	3,172	35,919
TOTAL	76,700	9,694	16,009	19,491	21,444	23,794	26,100	27,172	25,556	24,484	22,178	21,297	313,919
PAYMENTS													
Raw materials	2,800	4,375	5,950	6,300	6,650	7,700	8,225	8,225	7,000	6,825	6,300	6,125	76,475
Wages & NI	3,500	3,500	3,500	3,500	3,500	3,500	3,500	3,500	3,500	3,500	3,500	3,500	42,000
Rent	1,200	1,200	1,200	1,200	1,200	1,200	1,200	1,200	1,200	1,200	1,200	1,200	14,400
Rates	200	200	200	200	200	200	200	200	200	200	200	200	2,400
Insurance	1,650			1,650			1,650			1,650			6,600
HLP	2,000	450			450			450			450		3,800
Telephone	650		350			350			350			350	2,050
Advertising	3,500	500	500	500	500	500	500	500	500	500	500	500	9,000
Office costs	465	465	465	465	465	465	465	465	465	465	465	465	5,580
Travel etc	200	200	200	200	200	200	200	200	200	200	200	200	2,400
Professional fees	2,500	500			500			500			500	250	4,750
Repairs	100	100	100	100	100	100	100	100	100	100	100	100	1,200
Other	100	100	100	100	100	100	100	100	100	100	100	100	1,200
Capital	40,000		5,000	5,000		5,000	5,000		5,000				55,000
Bank charges	850	150			150			150			150		1,450
Loan repayments	250	250	250	250	250	250	250	250	250	250	250	250	3,000
Interest	150	150	150	150	150	150	150	150	150	150	150	150	1,800
Drawings	1,500	1,500	1,500	1,500	1,500	1,500	1,500	1,500	1,500	1,500	1,500	1,500	18,000
Tax													
VAT	9,155	1,171	1,341	2,216	1,569	1,648	2,553	1,845	1,525	2,308	1,508	1,416	28,255
VAT to C & E	0			(7,139)			4,170			5,780			2,811
TOTAL	70,770	14,811	15,806	16,192	17,484	17,863	29,764	19,335	17,040	29,729	17,073	16,306	282,171
BALANCE	5,930	(5,117)	203	3,298	3,960	5,931	(3,664)	7,837	8,516	(5,224)	5,106	4,991	
BANK BALANCE	5,930	813	1,016	4,314	8,274	14,205	10,542	18,379	26,895	21,651	26,757	31,748	31,748

This cash flow forecast has been prepared by Phil Stone of Parkstone Management Consultancy with information provided by Britannia Engineering. No responsibility can be accepted for its accuracy.

Because of the fact that you are showing credit sales in the month in which they are made you are also attributing the profit on those sales to that month. Profit is, however, only received when the actual cash has been received. Up until that time the profit element of the sales is still contained within your debtor figure in your balance sheet.

Linking income to cash flow

For reasons outlined above it is essential that you use the cash flow forecasts and the profit and loss forecasts in conjunction with each other. They cannot be used in isolation to judge the financial performance of the business. Only by meeting your sales targets will you achieve your profitability targets. In the same way, only once you have collected the cash from the sales will those profits be available to be spent. In the interim they are, therefore, both hypothetical figures.

> **TIP**
>
> Remember, profits do not mean that you hold that amount in cash In the same way, until you receive cash from your customers you have not made a profit on the sale.

Allocating expenses

The final point that you need to remember when compiling your forecasted profit and loss account is that not all items in the cash flow forecast will be included. You will only include items that are directly related to trading activity. You will not include within your business income items such as:

◆ capital introduced
◆ loans received.

Likewise, on the expenditure side you will not include such items as:

◆ funds used for the purchase of fixed assets.

SAMPLE PROFIT AND LOSS FORECAST

	Sep 01 £	Oct 01 £	Nov 01 £	Dec 01 £	Jan 02 £	Feb 02 £	Mar 02 £	Apr 02 £	May 02 £	Jun 02 £	Jul 02 £	Aug 02 £	Total £
TURNOVER													
Total Management Sales	47,500	47,500	47,500	20,000	20,000	47,500	177,000	-	47,500	70,500	70,500	70,500	666,000
IT Sales	11,878	11,878	11,878	11,878	11,878	11,878	11,878	11,878	11,878	11,878	11,878	11,878	142,536
	59,378	**59,378**	**59,378**	**31,878**	**31,878**	**59,378**	**188,878**	**11,878**	**59,378**	**82,378**	**82,378**	**82,378**	**808,536**
DIRECT COSTS													
Purchases	7,601	7,602	7,602	7,602	7,602	7,602	7,602	7,602	7,602	7,602	7,602	7,602	91,223
Sub Contract	641	642	641	642	641	642	641	641	642	641	642	641	7,697
	8,242	**8,244**	**8,243**	**8,244**	**8,243**	**8,244**	**8,243**	**8,243**	**8,244**	**8,243**	**8,244**	**8,243**	**98,920**
GROSS PROFIT	51,136	51,134	51,135	23,634	23,635	51,134	180,635	3,635	51,134	74,135	74,134	74,135	709,616
OVERHEADS													
Directors' Remuneration	5,226	5,226	5,226	5,226	5,226	5,226	5,225	5,226	5,226	5,226	5,226	5,226	62,711
Wages & Salaries	17,826	17,826	17,826	21,093	21,093	23,892	23,893	23,893	23,893	23,893	23,893	23,893	262,914
Rent	1,085	1,085	1,085	1,085	1,085	1,085	1,085	1,085	1,085	1,085	1,085	1,085	13,020
Training	-	3,054			3,054			3,054			3,054		12,216
Telephone	1,027	1,027	1,027	1,027	1,027	1,027	1,027	1,027	1,027	1,027	1,027	1,027	12,324
Printing and Stationery	469	469	469	469	469	469	469	469	469	469	469	469	5,628
Postage & Packaging	159	159	159	159	159	159	159	159	159	159	159	159	1,908
Equipment Rental	544	544	544	665	755	775	775	775	775	775	775	775	8,477
Insurance	673	673	673	673	673	673	673	673	673	673	673	673	8,076
Motor Expenses	2,260	2,260	2,260	2,260	2,260	2,260	2,260	2,260	2,260	2,260	2,260	2,260	27,120
Travel and Subsistence	1,356	1,356	1,356	1,356	1,356	1,356	1,356	1,356	1,356	1,356	1,356	1,356	16,272
Advertising	3,164	3,413	3,413	3,413	3,413	3,413	3,413	3,413	3,413	3,413	3,413	3,413	40,707
Entertainment	212	212	212	212	212	212	212	212	212	212	212	212	2,544
Legal and Professional	307	307	307	307	307	307	307	307	307	307	307	307	3,684
General Expenses	812	812	812	812	812	812	812	812	812	812	812	812	9,744
Depreciation	94	94	93	94	94	94	93	94	94	94	93	94	1,125
	35,214	**38,517**	**35,462**	**38,851**	**41,995**	**41,760**	**41,759**	**44,815**	**41,761**	**41,761**	**44,814**	**41,761**	**488,470**
OPERATING PROFIT	15,922	12,617	15,673	(15,217)	(18,360)	9,374	138,876	(41,180)	9,373	32,374	29,320	32,374	221,146
INTEREST EXPENSE													
Overdraft Interest	724	594	509	353	382	587	607	132	-	-	-	-	3,888
	724	**594**	**509**	**353**	**382**	**587**	**607**	**132**	**-**	**-**	**-**	**-**	**3,888**
NET PROFIT	**15,198**	**12,023**	**15,164**	**(15,570)**	**(18,742)**	**8,787**	**138,269**	**(41,312)**	**9,373**	**32,374**	**29,320**	**32,374**	**217,258**
CUMULATIVE	15,198	27,221	42,385	26,815	8,073	16,860	155,129	113,817	123,190	155,564	184,884	217,258	217,258

SAMPLE CASH FLOW FORECAST

	Sep 01 £	Oct 01 £	Nov 01 £	Dec 01 £	Jan 02 £	Feb 02 £	Mar 02 £	Apr 02 £	May 02 £	Jun 02 £	Jul 02 £	Aug 02 £	Total £
RECEIPTS													
Invoiced Sales	69,769	69,769	69,769	69,769	37,457	37,457	69,769	221,932	13,957	69,769	96,794	96,794	923,005
	69,769	**69,769**	**69,769**	**69,769**	**37,457**	**37,457**	**69,769**	**221,932**	**13,957**	**69,769**	**96,794**	**96,794**	**923,005**
PAYMENTS													
Invoiced Costs	18,663	22,503	29,466	22,796	22,939	29,713	23,069	23,068	29,737	23,069	23,068	29,738	297,829
Directors Remuneration	4,666	4,666	4,666	4,666	4,666	4,666	4,666	4,666	4,666	4,666	4,666	4,666	55,992
Wages & Salaries	15,916	15,916	15,916	18,833	18,833	21,333	21,333	21,333	21,333	21,333	21,333	21,333	234,745
Overdraft Interest	724	594	509	353	382	587	607	132					3,888
PAYE/NI	2,210	2,470	2,470	2,470	2,820	2,820	3,119	3,119	3,120	3,120	3,120	3,120	33,978
VAT	-	19,815	-	-	15,477	-	-	38,042	-	-	15,900	-	89,234
	42,179	**65,964**	**53,027**	**49,118**	**65,117**	**59,119**	**52,794**	**90,360**	**58,856**	**52,188**	**68,087**	**58,857**	**715,666**
NET CASH FLOW	**27,590**	**3,805**	**16,742**	**20,651**	**(27,660)**	**(21,662)**	**16,975**	**131,572**	**(44,899)**	**17,581**	**28,707**	**37,937**	**207,339**
OPENING BANK	(101,042)	(73,452)	(69,647)	(52,905)	(32,254)	(59,914)	(81,576)	(64,601)	66,971	22,072	39,653	68,360	(101,042)
CLOSING BANK	(73,452)	(69,647)	(52,905)	(32,254)	(59,914)	(81,576)	(64,601)	66,971	22,072	39,653	68,360	106,297	106,297

The final point to remember when compilin0g your profit and loss account forecasts is that, unlike in the cash flow forecasts, you will also exclude VAT. Although this does relate to funds that flow into and out of your business it has no reflection whatsoever on profitability.

In order to make the sample profit and loss forecast on page 132 actually mean something I have also included the cash flow forecast (on page 133) on which the figures have been based. The figures relating to expenditure have, however, been combined and are referred to as invoiced items.

THE BALANCE SHEET

The last component of your forecasted accounts is the balance sheet. All too often, however, it is totally ignored. This is a fundamental mistake because you can only identify the individual components of working capital by preparing a forecasted balance sheet.

This means that without such a forecast, you cannot identify the following:

- ◆ stock levels held
- ◆ debtors outstanding
- ◆ creditors outstanding.

Without such information you could find that you are running your business without sufficient liquidity. For example, you may be holding too much stock which in turn means that you are using cash unnecessarily. By the same token, you may have insufficient money due from debtors to meet your ongoing liability to your creditors. Either of these situations could be distorting your cash flow forecast. Once again, therefore, you need to be looking at the balance sheet forecasts in conjunction with your cash flow and profit and loss forecasts.

New business

With a new business, the opening balance sheet will consist of the assets to be introduced. In some cases this may be as simple as merely showing the cash injected by the owner which is then represented by a cash balance in the bank. This will, of course, also be shown in the cash flow forecasts. In other cases, where fixed assets are to be introduced, these will only appear in the balance sheet. They do not involve any movement of cash.

Once the business starts trading, the balance sheet will start to reflect the true trading position with the inclusion of the other elements of working capital. Hopefully, over time, it will also include the profit that the business is making.

Existing business

For an existing business, the forecasted balance sheets will include opening balances that are based on previous trading performance. These will bring forward the opening balances for all assets and liabilities. As with all the financial forecasts, the balance sheet for an existing company will be a lot easier to project than that of a new business.

> **TIP**
>
> Once you have established a trading history you can use the historic trends to formulate future forecasted financial information.

Sample balance sheet forecast

To help you identify the individual figures, a sample balance sheet appears on page 136 based on the profit and loss and cash flow forecasts that were used in the previous section.

SAMPLE BALANCE SHEET FORECAST

	Opening £	Sep 01 £	Oct 01 £	Nov 01 £	Dec 01 £	Jan 02 £	Feb 02 £	Mar 02 £	Apr 02 £	May 02 £	Jun 02 £	Jul 02 £	Aug 02 £
FIXED ASSETS													
Fixtures and Fittings	6,000	6,000	6,000	6,000	6,000	6,000	6,000	6,000	6,000	6,000	6,000	6,000	6,000
Accumulated Depreciation	(1,500)	(1,594)	(1,688)	(1,781)	(1,875)	(1,969)	(2,063)	(2,156)	(2,250)	(2,344)	(2,438)	(2,531)	(2,625)
	4,500	**4,406**	**4,312**	**4,219**	**4,125**	**4,031**	**3,937**	**3,844**	**3,750**	**3,656**	**3,562**	**3,469**	**3,375**
CURRENT ASSETS													
Bank									66,971	22,072	39,653	68,360	106,297
Trade Debtors	55,812	55,812	55,812	55,812	23,500	23,500	55,812	207,975	-	55,812	82,837	82,837	82,837
Other Debtors									1,939				
	55,812	**55,812**	**55,812**	**55,812**	**23,500**	**23,500**	**55,812**	**207,975**	**68,910**	**77,884**	**122,490**	**151,197**	**189,134**
CREDITORS DUE WITHIN ONE YEAR													
Bank	101,042	73,452	69,647	52,905	32,254	59,914	81,576	64,601	30,150	24,689	25,895	30,691	25,228
Trade Creditors	18,663	23,710	28,799	23,336	24,686	29,586	24,149	25,355	3,120	8,088	19,020	13,518	24,450
Other Creditors	15,034	22,285	8,884	15,832	18,297	4,385	11,591	41,161					
	134,739	**119,447**	**107,330**	**92,073**	**75,237**	**93,885**	**117,316**	**131,117**	**33,270**	**32,777**	**44,915**	**44,209**	**49,678**
NET CURRENT ASSETS	(78,927)	(63,635)	(51,518)	(36,261)	(51,737)	(70,385)	(61,504)	76,858	35,640	45,107	77,575	106,988	139,456
CREDITORS DUE AFTER ONE YEAR													
TOTAL NET ASSETS	**(74,427)**	**(59,229)**	**(47,206)**	**(32,042)**	**(47,612)**	**(66,354)**	**(57,567)**	**80,702**	**39,390**	**48,763**	**81,137**	**110,457**	**142,831**
CAPITAL & RESERVES													
Capital	30,000	30,000	30,000	30,000	30,000	30,000	30,000	30,000	30,000	30,000	30,000	30,000	30,000
Retained Earnings	(104,427)	(89,229)	(77,206)	(62,042)	(77,612)	(96,354)	(87,567)	50,702	9,390	18,763	51,137	80,457	112,831
	(74,427)	**(59,229)**	**(47,206)**	**(32,042)**	**(47,612)**	**(66,354)**	**(57,567)**	**80,702**	**39,390**	**48,763**	**81,137**	**110,457**	**142,831**

14

Looking at Grants and Subsidies

There is a substantial amount of financial assistance available to small businesses. Unfortunately, a great deal of this potential finance is missed purely because of ignorance of the schemes. Some people do not seem to wish to discuss their plans to establish a new business and so they can never receive appropriate help and advice.

APPLYING FOR GRANTS

The overriding principle for obtaining grants and other forms of financial assistance is that you must make your application, and have the assistance agreed, before you start your business. Unfortunately, a lot of businesses miss out because they do not follow this simple rule.

It is absolutely essential that you research the position thoroughly. Some grants are reliant upon either jobs being created or investment in new plant and machinery. Others have no restrictions whatsoever and are available purely by making a simple application.

> **TIP**
>
> Do not start your business then look for grants – research the position regarding potential grants as part of your initial research into your business idea.

Local government assistance

Most Local Authorities offer a range of incentives and grants for businesses to create jobs in their area. Some new businesses overlook this source of funding on the basis that they are creating no new jobs. This is factually incorrect. If you are starting your own business you are, at the very least, creating a new job for yourself.

You should contact the Economic Development Office within your Local Authority to find out what you may be eligible for because there will be some diversity across the UK. To give you some specific examples, however, the following schemes are available from the City of Sunderland Council:

◆ **Rent relief grant**s – available for between 25% and 50% of the rent payable for the first year of a new lease.
◆ **Basic services grants** – a 50% grant is available for the provision of new and essential services including electricity, gas or drainage work.
◆ **Interest relief grants** – amounting to 5% per annum for up to two years of the value of loans used to purchase machinery or buildings for industrial use.
◆ **Removal grants** – available to cover up to 50% of eligible costs incurred to move to industrial premises in the city.
◆ **Trainee employment grants** – grants are awarded to cover 75% of wages of new trainees in the first year and 25% in the second year.
◆ **Exhibition grants** – to cover 50% of the costs of exhibiting at a recognised trade exhibition outside the North East up to a maximum of £5,000.
◆ **Commercial Premises' Improvement and Security Grants** – of between 50% and 75% of eligible work on premises in specific regeneration areas of the City.

> **TIP**
>
> Find out what is available from your Local Authority and make any application for a grant as soon as you can. You do not need to have actually started your business before you apply provided you at least have a business plan.

For obvious reasons, all these grants have eligibility criteria, in addition to which they are entirely discretionary. This effectively means that even if you do qualify you may still not receive the funding because the council simply may not have any money left for the scheme.

Central government assistance

Through the Small Business Service, the Government offers a number
of schemes which can provide assistance in terms of either grants or
awards. The three main schemes are:

◆ Regional Selective Assistance (RSA)
◆ Regional Enterprise Grant (REG)
◆ Research and Development Grant.

Regional Selective Assistance

RSA is a discretionary scheme aimed at attracting investment and
creating or safeguarding jobs in selected areas of the UK. Grants are
available for qualifying projects with total project expenditure in excess of
£500,000 and can range from 5% to 15% of the fixed project costs. Each
application is individually assessed and the actual amount of the grant
will depend on the area, the project, and the number of jobs involved.

Regional Enterprise Grant

REG is also available only in selected areas of the UK and there are
variations in the eligibility criteria depending on location. The grant is
available up to a maximum of £75,000 on projects which involve up to
£500,000 of capital investment. In general, high growth businesses
seeking to maximise value added projects with quality output are given
a preference.

Research and Development Grant

Previously known as the SMART scheme this initiative provides grants
to help individuals and small and medium-sized businesses to research
and develop technologically innovative products and processes. Please

note that this grant is only available in England. Scotland, Wales and Northern Ireland have entirely separate initiatives.

There are four project areas:

◆ Micro Projects – simple low cost development projects lasting no more than 12 months. The output should be a simple prototype of the product or process. A grant of up to £20,000 is available to businesses with fewer than 10 employees.

◆ Research Projects – typically involve planned research or critical investigation lasting between 6 and 18 months. The result could be new scientific or technical knowledge that may be useful in developing a new product or process. A grant of up to £75,000 is available to businesses with fewer than 50 employees.

◆ Development Projects – involve the shaping of industrial research into a pre-production prototype of a technologically innovative product or process. A grant of up to £200,000 is available for businesses with fewer than 250 employees.

◆ Exceptional Projects – involve technology developments which have higher costs. These projects are likely to generate much wider economic benefits and must be recognised as of strategic importance for a technology or industrial sector. A grant of up to £500,000 is available.

TIP

Guidance notes and eligibility criteria for all three of the schemes above are available free of charge from the Dti.

In addition to the four main schemes above a further scheme, Investigating an Innovative Idea Grant is also available to businesses to help develop their ideas by working with external experts.

Developing new products, processes or services can be a complex process and not all businesses will have the skills or knowledge to manage the process effectively. Under this scheme a mentor is appointed to help identify areas where the business requires additional expertise to deveop an action plan to implement the idea.

Further details of all the above schemes can be obtained from the Dti Business Support Directory available free of charge on their website.

European assistance

Grants may be available from the European Union through the European Structural Funds. These include:

◆ European Regional Development Fund (ERDF)
◆ European Social Fund (ESF).

The criteria for obtaining such grants is decided by the members of the European Union and the actual amount available, and indeed, the member states which can benefit, are subject to constant review. At the present, the UK will receive over £10 billion for regeneration and economic development for the years 2000 to 2006. Plans have recently been announced for the European Structural Funds to be continued from 1 January 2007 although full details of the new initiatives are unlikely to be available until 2006.

> **TIP**
>
> European grants are extremely complicated and if you consider that you may be eligible you need to seek specialist advice – approach your Business Link in the first instance.

The Dti co-ordinates the administration of the available funds throughout the UK in conjunction with the Scottish, Welsh and Northern Ireland Offices and in England through the Local Government Offices.

You need to be aware that grants from the European Union are sometimes only considered by committees which meet once a year.

This can mean a substantial delay to your project because without approval no money can be spent.

KNOWING THE DIFFICULTIES

With the exception of the grants and assistance available from your Local Authority, which are relatively straightforward, you need to consider carefully whether the time and effort that you will put into making a grant application is actually worthwhile.

The process can be extremely long and drawn out and you can be sure that you will face a number of hurdles on the way. A word of warning at this stage. If you are approached by a company who state that they can help you identify and obtain grants in return for an up-front fee you need to be very wary. A number of such scam operations have been seen in the past where businesses have lost a considerable amount of money.

Advice on obtaining grants is freely available through the network of Business Links and other support organisations. In some locations, there is actually someone from the Dti within the offices of the Business Link with whom you can informally discuss your plans to see what may be available.

Meeting the criteria

Invariably there are very strict criteria involved in actually receiving a grant. You must understand exactly what is involved before you make an application. Some grants only relate to capital expenditure on fixed assets and others will allow the full project costs, including any working capital element to be included in the calculations.

> **TIP**
>
> If you receive an approach from any organisation offering to obtain grants for you then you should give their details to your local Dti office.

Always read carefully the literature that comes with the application forms. This will tell you how and when the application should be made, what supporting documentation will be required – for example a full business plan and financial projections for three years – and give clear guidelines on the amount that can be claimed.

Completing the application

Some application forms for grants are extremely complicated, especially those from Central Government and the European Union. It is vitally important that the application is completed correctly. In addition, you must remember that most grants are only available as 'gap' funding, i.e. when the finance cannot be obtained elsewhere and the project cannot be completed without the grant.

Unfortunately a lot of businesses assume that if they are investing money they should be eligible for a grant. That may have been the case some years ago but policy guidelines have changed. You must demonstrate the actual need for the grant. Even if you do qualify you must remember that most grants are discretionary.

It is most strongly recommended that if you are applying for a grant you should seek professional help with completing the application. Advisors can help you to ensure that your application is made as attractive and realistic as possible.

Waiting for the answer

Having made your application you will be in a state of limbo. Under normal circumstances, most projects cannot be commenced until the grant application has been approved. This means that you cannot do anything, or spend any money, on the project at all.

The actual time-scale following receipt of your application and receiving an answer can vary considerably. In many cases, the time taken is in direct proportion to the amount of grant that you are seeking. Remember that you are dealing with bureaucracy and should be prepared for a long wait.

> **TIP**
>
> Following receipt of your application the grant provider is likely to want to visit you and discuss your proposals further – make sure that you are absolutely prepared for the meeting.

Your application for a grant may be scaled down. You can be certain that your application will be scrutinised thoroughly and if the grant provider considers that cost savings can be made in any area of your application they will insist upon them. When, and if, you get a positive response to your grant application it may also be subject to a number of terms and conditions.

Actually getting the money

On the assumption that your grant application has been successful, actually getting the money can also be a long and drawn-out process. In many cases, the money may need to be spent first and receipts provided before the grant can be obtained. This in itself can be a major hurdle to overcome, especially where the grant is for a substantial sum.

Where other terms and conditions have been imposed, for example job creation, you may also need to prove that such jobs have been created before the grant will be paid. The number of terms and conditions will vary on an individual basis.

> **TIP**
>
> If any terms and conditions are attached to the grant you need to ensure that they are fulfilled as quickly as possible to enable you to make your claim.

You can see why I have given the advice that you need to think carefully about making an application for a grant. It is not an easy process and it can involve some pain along the way. In addition, many grants are taxable and the benefits can therefore be substantially reduced.

LOOKING FOR LOCAL HELP

There are a large range of organisations that offer help and advice to their members on running a business, such as the Forum of Private Business and the Federation of Small Business. Details of these and other organisations are contained in the Useful Contacts section at the end of this book.

There has also been a substantial increase in the private and 'not for profit' sector of organisations that provide localised help and assistance, usually with the support of both the Local Authority and Business Link.

> **TIP**
>
> Make sure that you check in your local Yellow Pages under the Business Enterprise Agenices for local organisations that can offer assistance.

Business support organisations

Financial grants from business support organisations, for example the Business Links, have been substantially reduced in recent years and are only generally available in small amounts, somewhere between £100 and £250. The vast majority of the assistance that they provide comes in a non-financial form.

The situation does, however, remain under constant review and your local office will give you advice on exactly what may be available. In some cases financial support can be received in terms of rent reductions on office or other units operated by the Business Link.

Business Links will also normally offer training facilities on a subsidised or free of charge basis. A number of different courses are offered catering both for the owner of a business and indeed any staff employed by a business. Whilst these are not a direct form of financial assistance they do mean that you may have no financial outlay in order to gain new skills yourself or to train your staff.

The Prince's Trust

If you are looking to start your own business and are between 18 and 30 years of age and presently unemployed you may be able to receive assistance from The Prince's Trust. This assistance can take a number of different forms including:

◆ a low interest loan of up to £5,000
◆ test marketing grants of up to £250
◆ grants of up to £1,500 in special circumstances
◆ advice from an appointed 'business mentor' during the first three years
◆ extra support including discounted exhibition space and specialist advice.

The Prince's Trust operates through a number of area offices throughout the UK. To qualify for help you need to have a viable business idea and have been refused all or some of the finance from any other source.

> **TIP**
>
> If you are aged 18 to 25 and are looking to start your own business you should approach your local Job Centre to see if there are any specialist schemes available to you.

15
Writing Your Business Plan

In simple terms, a business plan is a written summary of what you hope to accomplish by being in business and how you will accomplish those objectives. It must contain clear goals and objectives with an explanation of how you intend to manage all your resources, i.e. premises, equipment and staff, as well as finances in order to achieve those goals and objectives.

A business plan should be seen as an ongoing document that can never be completed. When it seems complete a number of factors can make it immediately out of date, such as slippage in collecting money owed, or delays in receipt of supplies of raw materials.

> **TIP**
> Time spent on a business plan is well spent – failures in planning can lead to overall failure.

A good business plan for an existing business demonstrates that careful consideration has been given to the business's ongoing development. In the case of a new business it shows that the entrepreneur has completed sufficient research and has the necessary skills and vision to succeed.

WHY DO I NEED A BUSINESS PLAN?

A formal business plan should be seen as an important management tool by all businesses irrespective of size. It serves four critical functions:

◆ It helps to clarify, focus and research the development of the business or project.

147

◆ It provides a framework for the business strategy to be undertaken over the coming years in order for the business to develop.

◆ The document can be used as a basis for discussion with third parties who have either a potential or an existing interest in the business, such as shareholders, banks, or other investors.

◆ It sets goals and objectives against which actual performance can be measured and reviewed.

If you are seeking external support to start your business, the business plan is probably the most important sales document you will ever produce. It gives you the only opportunity to sell the concept behind your business and raise the funds to achieve success. Even if you do not require external funding, the whole planning process of thinking, discussing, researching, analysing and evaluating options forces you to understand more clearly what you want to achieve and how and when you are going to achieve it.

WHERE DO I START?

In exactly the same way that no two businesses are alike, no two business plans will be identical. The important thing to remember is that a business plan must be tailored to meet the individual situation. Most business plans, however, follow a tried and tested structure with sub-headings to cover all eventualities.

A sample business plan template, with guidance on content is given at the end of this chapter. For now we will concentrate on the general style and content that you should follow when structuring your plan. The business plan will be divided into individual sections, and these can be grouped together in the overall structure into three parts covering the areas previously outlined:

◆ where you are now
◆ where you want to be
◆ how you are going to get there.

Opening with a synopsis

To the reader of your plan the synopsis will be the most important element. This could be your one and only chance to make a favourable impression on your target audience and you must not waste it. The synopsis must contain sufficient information in a concise format to make your audience want to discover more about your plans.

The synopsis should not normally be longer than one page and it should contain the following information:

◆ the background to your business or your business idea
◆ an outline of your proposals
◆ what you need from your audience.

> **TIP**
>
> Because the synopsis is a summary of the entire business plan you must have completed the entire plan before you can attempt to write this section.

This final part is very important. If you are putting a proposal to a potential funder you must tell them what it is you want from them and how it will be repaid. Whilst this will be contained in detail in the body of the business plan it needs to be clearly outlined from the beginning.

Identify where you are now

The first part of your business plan should detail exactly where you are now. For a new business this will involve details of why you are considering starting your business together with your own business or other experience. It will also include an outline of the products or services that you will provide.

The most important section within this part of your business plan will provide an analysis of the market in which you propose to operate. This section will need to be extremely comprehensive to demonstrate that you have done your research and understand the market conditions. It is likely that this will take some time to write and you should not be in any hurry to complete it. If you miss a critical aspect of the market your business could fail before you even become established.

Define where you are going

The middle section of your business plan will identify where you want your business to be in the future. The marketing strategy in this part of your plan is extremely important, and must detail in some depth exactly how you propose competing in your target market.

TIP

Check and double check the contents of your business plan – any silly mistakes will only demonstrate your lack of attention to detail.

You will also need to give details of the way in which you propose to start your business, summarising the financial forecasts that you have prepared detailing your potential income and expenditure. The actual forecasts will be included as an appendix to the business plan. It is important that your words and figures match. If, for example, you state that your targeted first year turnover will be £x then your financial forecasts should not show £y.

Explain your strategy to achieve your objectives

The final part of your business plan will explain how you are going to establish your business. It will define the resources that you need in terms of people, premises and equipment, and the funding that the business will require. In this funding section you should incorporate the money that you are going to provide, together with where it is going to come from, and the finance that you require from external sources.

In conclusion, this part of your plan should deal with a risk evaluation; in other words, the action that you can take if things do not go to plan. By thinking through what could go wrong you can be one step ahead of any problems and have appropriate contingency strategies in place to deal with them.

MAKE SURE THE CONTENT IS UNDERSTANDABLE

Entrepreneurs sometimes get so mixed up in commercial jargon that they forget that someone outside of their industry may have no idea what they are talking about. It is essential when writing the business plan that you avoid the use of jargon, or, when it cannot be avoided, the meaning is clearly explained so that a layman can understand it.

> **TIP**
>
> Get a friend or relative to read your business plan – if they cannot understand any part of it then you will need to simplify the content.

Cover all the angles

The ideal business plan will be so thorough that the potential funder will have few, if any, questions on your proposal. You need to cover all eventualities and make adequate provision for any unforeseen circumstances. It is, for example, acceptable to allow for some slippage in the receipt of debtor monies. Provided you can explain why you have built in such a contingency and that it is realistic it will not be criticised by the potential lender.

USE FACT NOT FICTION

Throughout the course of doing your research you will have discovered numerous facts and figures. You will no doubt have also unearthed the opinions and assertions of many people either connected or unconnected with your market. The important job that you now face is to sort out the fact from the fiction.

Within your business plan you will make a number of assumptions, not just related to the financial forecasts and it is important that you back up these assumptions with supporting facts.

The target audience for your business plan will need to be convinced that what you are telling them is true and the only way that you can do this is by presenting them with firm evidence.

At all costs, avoid waffle and unsubstantiated claims. For example, there is little point in describing your target market as 'increasing substantially year on year'. What does that actually mean? Has it perhaps now reached saturation? Why should it grow any further?

If you are going to make a claim such as this then back it up with hard facts and evidence. For example, 'the market has increased from £xm to £ym over the last two years, and, according to research carried out by Anytown University, growth will continue at a rate of z% per annum for the foreseeable future'.

TIP

If you are going to use facts or statistics from a third party source make sure that the source is well recognised, for example the National Audit Office, and not from somewhere obscure and possibly out of date.

This demonstrates to your target audience that you have:

◆ done your research
◆ understood the results
◆ converted this information into an opportunity for your business.

Remember, if the target audience is sufficiently interested in your business plan they may well do some research of their own in order to substantiate your claims. You need to make sure that the facts that they obtain will match your own.

Always tell the truth

The importance of your integrity and reputation as an entrepreneur cannot be over-emphasised. If you misrepresent the facts, or even worse, blatantly lie about any part of your background or your business history, you will lose the confidence and trust of potential or existing funders. In some circumstances you could even face personal liability despite operating your business under the auspices of a limited liability company.

Telling the truth can sometimes be hard, but in all cases, especially when dealing with potential funders, it is the only option. If you fail to provide information which is relevant to your business proposal this could be seen as blatant misrepresentation. Even if this fact is not discovered until some time later, the damage will have already been done.

> **TIP**
>
> Damage to your reputation and integrity could be impossible to repair – once you have lost someone's trust they may not want to do business with you again.

WHAT TO INCLUDE

Your business plan needs to answer all the potential questions that your target audience may have. Even if the plan is just for internal use it needs to be presented in an easy-to-read and logical format to demonstrate that you do know what you are talking about.

If you are using the plan to raise finance the trick is to put yourself in the position of the potential funder. You know the sort of questions you have already asked yourself when doing your research and compiling the SWOT and PESTE analyses. What you need to ensure is that the business plan answers all of these questions.

A potential funder will not be impressed if they have a question that you are unable to answer. All that this demonstrates to them is that your research is inadequate and based on this fact alone they may simply decline your proposition. You may only get one chance, so get it right first time.

You need to be aware that the overall size of your business plan should be relevant to its proposed purpose although that does not necessarily mean that the larger the funding requirement, the larger the business plan. It also does not necessarily follow that a well presented business plan will have a greater chance of success.

WHAT NOT TO INCLUDE

Sometimes it is difficult to decide exactly what should and what should not be included in a business plan. The main point to remember is that whilst it needs to be concise, it also needs to be clear and uncluttered.

If you include irrelevant material it can make the plan very difficult to read and this will not help your cause. For example, as part of your research you may have completed a survey of potential customers. It is not necessary to include all the answer sheets in the plan, but it is relevant to include a brief summary of your analysis.

As another example, you may have obtained research from a company such as Mintel which outlines in detail the exact market conditions. Do not include the actual document, but make reference to the findings in summarised format. If the target audience requires sight of the actual research then they will ask you for it.

Another mistaken inclusion is the curriculum vitae of the entrepreneur which often runs to many pages but basically gives no relevant information. If you were seeking employment this may be necessary but within a business plan your examination achievements many years ago at school are of no relevance whatsoever. A one-page summary directly relating to your business skills, experience and qualifications is more than enough.

THE CONTENTS OF A GOOD BUSINESS PLAN

Your business plan should be divided into clear sections. These will present the information in a logical format and make the plan easy to read and understand. Ideally you should also number the individual paragraphs. If the plan is being submitted to a potential funder this will make it easier for them when recording their file notes.

Section One – Contact details

This should be no more than a single page and contain details of the business or trading name, the registered and trading address and contact name with telephone and fax numbers together with e-mail and website address if appropriate.

Section Two – Synopsis

A short synopsis of the business plan should be given, usually no more than a few paragraphs. The reader must be aware from the outset exactly what the plan is all about, what it has been written for, and what is being sought. If you are seeking funding you should state exactly how much, for what, and how long it will take to repay.

Section Three – Business background and history

You need to make sure that a full background to the business is provided covering:

◆ when the business was started

◆ how it has developed since then

◆ any significant mile stones or achievements

◆ any accreditation gained such as quality standard awards or awards from industrial or other bodies.

In the case of a new business where there is no background history then this section needs to include details of why the business is starting up and short details of the owner's own background and experience.

Section Four – The product

This section should give a precise description of exactly what it is that the business will be doing with specific details of any range of products or services.

It is also important that you outline what the products or services will do for the consumer, and what differentiates this product or service from those that may already be available in the market.

Section Five – Operational process

This section is only really appropriate to any firm that is involved in direct manufacturing of a product. If this is appropriate then full details of the exact procedures required from the basic ordering of raw materials right through all of the production stages to achieve the final finished product should be given.

If the process is long and complicated involving numerous production stages, then merely use a flow diagram and bullet points.

Section Six – Market analysis

For any business this is one of the most important sections of the business plan because it deals with the overall market and should establish exactly how the business specifically operates in that market.

Details should therefore be given with as much information as possible:

- the overall size of the market, both domestic and international
- trends within that market – supported by relevant figures
- specific details of direct competitors – who they are, what they do and how they compare
- market segmentation in terms of trade, retail, wholesale and mail order
- pricing expectations
- potential customers
- quality and service standards
- relevant legislation such as Health and Safety
- environmental concerns
- relevant independent market research information if available.

This can never be an exhaustive list and each business plan will require differing market analysis depending on the market in which the business operates.

Section Seven – Marketing strategy

Using the information gained from the market analysis the business can now start to formulate the marketing strategy, and the initial stage will probably involve the use of a SWOT analysis.

This will assist in formulating the marketing strategy around the five key components:

◆ **Customers and markets** – a clear understanding of the potential customers and markets needs to be shown. In other words, to whom are you going to sell your products or services?

◆ **Product** – what it is that the business will sell. Remember this has been covered previously and therefore only a brief description is necessary with comparisons to any existing products gleaned from the analysis.

◆ **Price** – how much will be charged and how this figure has been calculated. How does it compare to the competition and what sort of margin or mark-up has been used and why?

◆ **Promotion** – how will the business advertise its product or service and where. How much will it cost and over what period, i.e. will there be a large product launch campaign followed by smaller adverts in the following time periods?

◆ **Place** – where will the business operate from and why? How will the products be distributed and where will they be sold?

It is vitally important that the business achieves what is known as the correct 'marketing mix' within the strategy with all components correctly balanced.

Section Eight – The project

This section should give a short synopsis of the project which will in effect summarise the next few sections.

Details should be given of the reasons behind the project, exactly what it is and what benefits it will bring to the business such as cost savings. In addition to this, summarised details of job creation and capital expenditure should be outlined.

Most importantly of all, set out the finance required and exactly what that funding will be used for, i.e. working capital in terms of revenue expenditure or fixed capital for expenditure on assets such as premises and equipment.

Section Nine – Management structure

Where there are only a limited number of key personnel, as in the case of sole traders or small partnerships, a full background profile should be inserted here for every member of the management team. For larger organisations it is necessary to show a full management structure diagram clearly showing levels of responsibility and reporting lines.

In all cases, full details of all members of the management team should be given which clearly show the experience and skills that they bring to the business, and in the case of any anticipated new members of the team, exactly what skills will be necessary to do the job and whether in fact there is anyone being considered to fill the position.

Section Ten – Human resources

Full details should be set out here in table format of all staff presently employed together with projections for the required levels of staff over the next three years.

Where additional staff are required for the expansion of the business, details should be given of specific responsibilities and potential salary or wage. If the new members of staff are required in the short term, outline what efforts have been made to recruit, or indeed, if there is already a potential candidate.

Section Eleven – Premises and equipment

Existing businesses should give exact details of the present trading premises in terms of freehold, leasehold or rented, with details of monthly or annual rental payments, length of lease, review dates and possible market valuation.

New businesses will need to give details of proposed location and whether freehold, leasehold or rented, rental payments, proposed length of lease and likely start date.

Details of capital expenditure should also be given in table format for all equipment to be purchased over the life of the business plan, usually three years. If relevant, reasons for such purchases should be given especially where such new equipment will bring about cost savings or greater operational efficiency.

Section Twelve – Financial information

Summarised tables should be provided of any previous financial statements and the forecasted cash flow, profit and loss and balance sheets in order that comparisons can be seen in a simple logical format.

If the business is involved in importing or exporting, full details in terms of percentage sales and purchases should be given.

Section Thirteen - Funding requirement

If appropriate, set out details of existing finance available such as bank overdrafts. Also give specific details of the new finance being sought in terms of type of funding i.e. bank loan or increased overdraft, hire purchase, leasing, equity via either venture capital or business angel.

Set out the existing capital structure of the business in terms of issued share capital or owner's capital and whether this is to be changed. In the case of a new start business, details should also be given of the opening capital to be injected, and if relevant, the source of that injection whether it be in terms of cash or introduction of assets.

Finally, set out the timing and source of repayment. This is usually in terms of retained profits as evidenced by the profit and loss forecasts, or less frequently, in the case of equity capital provided by venture capitalists, the anticipated stock flotation timetable.

Section Fourteen – Risk evaluation

The final section of the business plan is devoted to a sensitivity analysis looking at what may happen in the event of variations in the business plan forecasts and what could be done to minimise the risk both to the business and the potential funder.

This must clearly demonstrate that all possible risks have been considered, such as a downturn in overall turnover or a reduced overall profit margin due perhaps to increased costs, and that within the business plan you have allowed for such risks with contingency strategies.

16 Raising Finance

Raising finance for your business should not be difficult provided you either have an existing profitable business or you have an idea for a new business that is feasible. Both of these aspects are important. If a lender is to finance your business they must be sure that you can meet the repayments. They are in business to lend money and make a profit.

Raising the right type of finance for your business is also important. There is little point in borrowing money on a short-term basis if you can only repay it over the long term. This is a common mistake that small businesses make. They utilise short-term finance, for example a bank overdraft, to finance long-term expenditure such as the purchase of a new vehicle. This then leads to a reduction in short-term finance for working capital which could, in some circumstances, lead to business failure. You must match the type of finance to the type of expenditure.

Your bank will probably be your first option to gain finance for your business, but we will also look at other alternatives in order that you can gain an overall picture of what may be available.

TIP

Never accept the first offer of finance – finance providers are in a very competitive market and if you have a good proposition you should always seek alternative quotations.

INVESTING YOUR OWN MONEY

Before you can even consider raising funds from external sources you must make your own investment. This investment takes two main forms:

- financial
- non-financial.

Financial investment, as the name suggests, is a direct injection of cash into your business. If you are operating as a limited liability company, this could take the form of share capital or director's loan. If you operate either as a sole trader or partnership, it will be classified as owner's or partner's capital.

The decision as to which type of business to operate can be complex. There are advantages and disadvantages to operating as a sole trader or as a partnership, or as a limited liability company. From the outset you need to seek professional advice on this aspect.

Non-financial investment is the introduction of assets that you may already own, such as motor vehicles and tools and equipment. These need to be carefully valued for inclusion in your financial records. If you are introducing assets into your business in this way you are advised to seek the help of an accountant. This will ensure that your assets are correctly valued and that they comply with any Inland Revenue guidelines.

Showing commitment

There are no hard and fast rules about how much of your own money you must invest in your business before you can gain finance. One of the important factors that the potential lender will be looking for is that you are showing a total commitment to your business.

> **TIP**
>
> Unless you are personally investing in your own business it is unlikely that you will gain the support of an external funder – they will not assume all the risk in you starting your business.

Gearing

Gearing is the relationship between your funds in the business, the owner's capital, and borrowed money or debt. Let us assume that your business has £5,000 capital and you are seeking £7,500 of borrowed funds. Gearing is calculated by dividing one by the other and can be expressed in one of two ways:

◆ gearing percentage – £7,500 ÷ £5,000 x 100 = 150%
◆ gearing ratio – £7,500 ÷ £5,000 = 1.5:1

This shows that for every £1 of capital there are debts of £1.50. Gearing of more than 100% is considered high. Gearing of less than 100% is considered low. This means that with low gearing the owner is shouldering the majority of the risk. Conversely, with high gearing, the lender is assuming more risk than the owner.

For a small business looking to raise finance, the lender will probably be looking for gearing as close to 100% as possible, although there is no 'perfect' gearing ratio and each proposition is considered on its merits.

It will also depend to a certain extent on the type of finance that you require. For short-term finance, for example a bank overdraft, it is likely that gearing of 100%, i.e. matching finance, will be possible. On the other hand, long-term lending may only require a small contribution from you. For example, the purchase of a vehicle may only require a 10% deposit from you, equating to a gearing ratio of 900%.

SHORT-TERM FINANCE

Quite obviously short-term finance is designed to be used and repaid in the short term. This is often referred to as working capital finance. It is used to finance working capital and pay creditors and is then itself repaid following receipt of funds from debtors. The most common form of short-term finance is provided by banks in the form of an overdraft.

Overdrafts

Whilst overdrafts may be the most common form of short-term finance they are also probably the most abused. They are often used for purchasing assets for which long-term finance should have been obtained. An overdraft is a revolving form of credit up to an agreed limit. This limit is agreed in advance and is then available for use, usually for a defined period normally ranging from a few months up to one year. You are then free to draw on that facility as and when required.

Overdrafts do not have any defined repayment date, although the bank will normally insist when granting the facility that it is repayable in full on demand. This does, of course, mean that it can be taken away just as quickly as it can be granted.

TIP
If you are granted an overdraft facility then make sure you stay within the agreed limit – exceed this limit and penal rates of interest in excess of 30% may be applied together with additional account charges.

Trade credit

Obtaining credit from your suppliers is also another easy form of short-term finance. It can also be the cheapest form of finance. You are, effectively, using other people's money to finance your business although no interest or other charges are payable. The terms of such credit can vary widely from a few weeks up to many months and will depend, in many cases, upon the particular type of business that you operate.

Having gained agreement to a credit account it is extremely important that you do not abuse that facility. It can just as easily be withdrawn, placing severe pressure on your cash flow. Always adhere to the agreed terms of the credit and make payment promptly when it is required.

Failure to pay on time could also render you liable to penalties. Always remember that the provisions of the Late Payment of Commercial Debt

TIP

Personal credit cards can also, at least initially, be used to gain credit for your business. There is absolutely nothing to stop you using them, although you will need to keep a careful track of the relevant records.

Act will also apply to debts that you owe. Bearing in mind the considerable statutory interest rate, the charges involved could represent a substantial amount and are therefore something that you should avoid at all costs. Of course, if your creditors start to charge you on this basis it is also likely that they will have already withdrawn your credit facility.

Trade credit is not something that is only available to established businesses. In these times of intense competition, suppliers need to be flexible in how they make their sales. Do not be put off by an initial refusal. Try another supplier and you may get a different answer.

Factoring

A factoring service enables you to bridge the gap between sending the invoice and actually receiving payment. It is specifically designed for small businesses, usually with turnover of at least £250,000 although sometimes lower limits are available. The factor will take over the running of your sales ledger and will issue statements and debtor reminders according to an agreed timetable.

Factoring your debts means that you can obtain an immediate advance against your outstanding debtors. This usually equates to a maximum of 80% of approved invoices. In this case, 'approved' means that the customers have been approved as debtors by the factoring company.

The advantages of factoring:
◆ It improves cash flow with a faster collection of trade debts.
◆ It removes the need to chase unpaid invoices.
◆ It is a simple process and insurance against bad debts may be available.

The disadvantages of factoring:

◆ Your customers know that you are using the factor – in some cases this does have a stigma attached to it.

◆ It can prove costly in overall terms.

◆ Once you have taken out a factoring arrangement it can be difficult to extricate yourself from the arrangement.

Invoice discounting

Invoice discounting operates on broadly the same principles as factoring but with two main differences:

◆ Control of the sales ledger is retained by you and you will therefore need to control the debtors and chase for late payment yourself.

◆ Because you retain control, the existence of the invoice discounting arrangement is not evident to your customers – it is entirely confidential.

Because the principles are broadly the same in each case, both factoring and invoice discounting share the same advantages and disadvantages. The only difference, of course, is the perception of your customers when, rather than dealing with you concerning their invoices, they deal with the factor.

TIP
If you are considering factoring or invoice discounting then you should seek advice from your accountant – both schemes can be very difficult to ever actually repay.

LONG-TERM FINANCE

If you are considering purchasing any form of fixed asset, for example, plant and machinery or vehicles, you must obtain long-term finance. In addition, it is prudent to obtain that finance on repayment terms linked to the likely life of the asset. For example, if you are purchasing an asset with a working life of three years, it would be prudent to repay the necessary finance over the same term. In most cases the lender will indeed insist upon this. It would be futile for them to lend you money over ten years for an asset that will only last for three years.

Loans

Business loans are available from a wide variety of sources and on a wide range of terms and conditions. Some are secured on assets of one kind or another and some are available on an unsecured basis. As with all forms of finance, you need to know and understand the exact conditions under which the loan is being made available.

One thing to look out for is early repayment penalties. Even if you do have the means to repay the loan early it could cost you extra in terms of a fee or penalty interest. Most loans are covered by the various consumer credit legislation. They now give you 'cooling off' periods and a lot of the somewhat dubious terms and conditions that were previously imposed have been made illegal.

The majority of business loans are provided by banks and are usually subject to a minimum amount of £1,000 and a maximum amount of £1m. Repayment terms are also flexible, depending upon the purpose of the loan and can range from a 12-month period up to 20 years.

In some circumstances it is also possible to arrange a capital repayment holiday where only the interest needs to be repaid for the defined term of the holiday. This can be advantageous for a new business in that it keeps expenditure down to a minimum whilst income is being built up from trade. This type of deferred repayment should be available regardless of whether you opt for a variable rate or a fixed rate loan.

TIP

You need to consider the options of fixed rate or variable rate very carefully – you do not want to tie yourself to a high rate loan when interest rates are generally reducing.

Variable rate loans

Variable rate loans are entirely flexible but you need to be aware that this can actually cause you problems if the base lending rate increases. The bank will usually review your outstanding loan on an annual basis and if the base rate has increased substantially during the past 12 months this can also lead to a substantial increase in your repayments.

On the other hand, the bank may be willing to extend the repayment time-scale to allow you additional time to pay off the loan. Either way your costs have increased and this can only come out of your business profits. It can also make budgeting very difficult.

Fixed rate loans

Fixed rate loans have three specific features which are designed to take away the uncertainty of using a variable rate loan:

◆ The interest rate for the entire period of the loan is fixed from the outset.
◆ The monthly repayments are fixed for the full term of the loan.
◆ The full term of the loan is also fixed.

This means that you know from the outset exactly how much your repayments will be each month and how long the loan will take to repay. This cannot vary throughout the entire period of the loan. As you might expect, however, there can be a financial cost for this certainty.

It is likely that the interest rate that you will be offered will be higher than a comparative interest rate for a variable rate loan. What you have to remember is that by offering the fixed rate the bank is having to make assumptions about how the base rate is likely to move in the future. In effect this additional cost is the premium that you have to pay to ensure financial stability.

Loan repayment tables

In order to help you establish the repayments necessary for any loan, a table appears below with various interest rates and repayment terms. In order to work out the monthly repayment for a loan you merely take the relevant cost from the table and multiply this figure by the amount of the loan that you require (divided by 1,000, so that £8,600, for example, becomes 8.6).

Please remember that these repayment tables can only provide a general guide to the repayments that will be required. The actual repayment amount will be based on when the bank charges the interest to the loan account. Some loans are charged interest monthly and others are charged quarterly. This is, of course, another aspect that you will need to consider when you are pricing the true cost of the loan.

You can only make a direct comparison of the true costs of borrowing money when you know the APR:

Years	Interest Rates					
	10%	12%	14%	16%	18%	20%
1	£87.92	£88.85	£89.79	£90.73	£91.68	£92.63
2	£46.14	£47.07	£48.01	£48.96	£49.92	£50.90
3	£32.27	£33.21	£34.18	£35.16	£36.15	£37.16
4	£25.36	£26.33	£27.33	£28.34	£29.37	£30.43
5	£21.25	£22.24	£23.27	£24.32	£25.39	£26.49
6	£18.53	£19.55	£20.61	£21.69	£22.81	£23.95
7	£16.60	£17.65	£18.74	£19.86	£21.02	£22.21
8	£15.17	£16.25	£17.37	£18.53	£19.72	£20.95
9	£14.08	£15.18	£16.33	£17.53	£18.76	£20.03
10	£13.22	£14.35	£15.53	£16.75	£18.02	£19.33

For example:

The repayment amount for a loan of £8,600 repayable over ten years at an interest rate of 12% = 8.6 x £14.35 = £123.41 per month.

The Small Firms Loan Guarantee Scheme

The Small Firms Loan Guarantee Scheme (SFLGS) is a joint venture operated by the Small Business Service (SBS) and a consortium of lenders including the high street banks. It is available to small businesses that have a viable business plan but who have been unable to raise a conventional loan. This may be because of a lack of security or business track record, or both.

Under the scheme the Government provides a guarantee to the participating funder against default by the borrower. The amount of this guarantee is 70% of the loan, although for businesses that have been trading for more than two years this increases to 85%. This therefore mitigates substantially the risk that the funder is taking in granting the loan.

The minimum amount of loan that can be considered is £5,000 and for a new start business the maximum is £100,000. For established businesses that have been trading for at least two years the maximum amount available rises to £250,000. Guarantees are available to cover loans repayable between two and ten years.

> **TIP**
>
> If you cannot provide any security for a bank loan, the Small Firms Loan Guarantee Scheme could provide you with finance – check with your bank to see if your business is eligible.

Hire purchase

Hire purchase is one of the most common forms of finance for individuals and it can be a very flexible form of finance for businesses.

You only have to walk down your local high street to see the range of hire purchase schemes that are available, some more expensive than others.

Hire purchase is an agreement to buy an asset, for example, a motor vehicle or computer equipment, with defined repayments over an agreed term. Depending upon the agreement, ownership of the asset may, or may not, pass to you immediately. Some agreements, for obvious reasons, do not allow ownership until all instalments have been paid.

Leasing

Leasing is an extremely flexible form of funding. A lease is negotiated with the lessor who acquires the asset that has been chosen by the lessee. The assets that can be leased are wide and varied. Photocopiers, computer systems, office furniture, motor vehicles, machine tools and heavy plant and equipment are all examples.

Leasing should be distinguished from hiring. Hiring requires the user to select an item from stock already held by the hirer. Leasing enables the lessee to select any item from any manufacturer or supplier. The choice is therefore unlimited. The leasing agreement will consequently be tailor-made for the actual asset involved.

There are three types of lease:
◆ finance lease
◆ operating lease
◆ contract hire.

Finance lease

With a finance lease, the lessor pays for the asset and becomes the owner. The lessee then pays a rental which covers the capital cost of the asset together with interest and service charges. The purpose of this type of lease is solely to provide finance to the lessee on the security of the asset. The lessee is responsible for all maintenance and insurance.

Operating lease

Operating leases are mainly undertaken by manufacturers of products that tend to be highly specialised or technical. The lease usually provides that the lessor is responsible for servicing, maintaining and updating the equipment. Operating leases can also enable the lessee to avoid some of the risks of ownership, for example, obsolescence.

Contract hire

Contract hire is similar to an operating lease. One of the most common uses of contract hire is to finance a fleet of motor vehicles. In this case, the lessor takes responsibility for the regular maintenance and servicing of the vehicles. The lessee merely has to consider the day-to-day fuel costs.

> **TIP**
>
> As with all forms of funding, make sure you check the true annual interest rate or APR that you are being charged – some forms of hire purchase and leasing can work out to be very expensive.

Soft loans

Soft loans are loans that are available on generous terms and at lower interest rates than would be charged commercially. Generally, they are provided through local Enterprise Agencies and are available where conventional funding, for example through a bank, cannot be obtained for any reason.

Enterprise Agencies are not-for-profit organisations which provide a wide variety of services to small businesses on a localised basis. The loan funds that they operate will be available on various terms and conditions, and, in some circumstances, they are only available to people within a certain age band.

In some cases, the provision of a soft loan can actually lead to further conventional funding being raised. Most soft loan fund managers take a personal interest in the businesses in which they invest and accordingly they provide a high level of support and advice. This involvement can give confidence to the traditional funders, i.e. bank managers, who know that a strict degree of control will be exercised.

This phenomenon is known as 'leverage'. The soft loan levers further funding and reduces the risks for both funders. In some cases, there are informal agreements between the managers who administer the soft loan funds and the high street banks. This works on the basis that the bank will match the amount of the loan that is made by the soft loan provider, usually up to an agreed maximum, in order that total funding for a project can be achieved on a shared basis.

GAINING EQUITY FINANCE

Most small businesses avoid equity at all costs on the basis that they want to maintain sole control. Most small business start-ups will not actually be able to gain equity funding, even if they want it, because providers of such capital are usually only interested in making a substantial investment. The normal criterion for most venture capitalists is a minimum equity investment of £250,000.

> **TIP**
>
> If you are seeking finance and equity is an option then you should not be afraid to offer a share in your business – owning part of a successful business is infinitely better than owning 100% of a business that has insufficient capital.

In some circumstances, however, especially where your own capital contribution is small and your borrowing requirement is large, equity funding will be essential as part of the overall package of funding.

For the start-up business there are two likely sources of equity funding:

◆ business angels

◆ venture capital.

Business angels

Business angels are high net worth individuals with a background of running their own successful business. Quite apart from considering that you have a sound proposal they will also want to take a very 'hands on' approach in the running of your business. This can be both an opportunity and a burden to you. You will be able to take advantage of their business expertise and acumen but they will expect to be involved in all decisions made concerning the business.

Most business angels will only invest in businesses located in close proximity to where they live. You may find that your local Business Link will have their own register of potential business angels but even if they do not they can point you in the right direction. As an alternative, you can use the services of the National Business Angels Network (NBAN).

Venture capital

Venture capital firms will only accept businesses with high growth potential that are managed by skilled, ambitious owners. There are a number of defined stages in the development of a business where venture capital could be considered:

Seed capital

Seed capital investments are usually made in businesses with a new high technology product that will provide real innovation, and accordingly high returns.

Start-up capital

Although most start-up businesses are typically small in size, there is an increasing number of multi-million-pound businesses being started. This is a result of the revolution caused by the Internet and the subsequent increase in the number of 'dot com' businesses being started. With the high number of such business failures, however, the venture capital funders will be more reticent about making such investments.

Expansion capital

This is by far the largest single use of venture capital accounting for over 50% of such investments. Funding is generally made available to finance increased production capacity, product development and marketing, and to provide additional working capital.

Finding a venture capitalist

All of the venture capitalists in the UK are represented by the British Venture Capital Association (BVCA). The BVCA publishes an annual directory of members which is available free of charge and lists venture capital firms as well as their investment preferences and full contact details.

> **TIP**
>
> You need to be aware that equity investors are looking for a significant return on their investment – returns in excess of 30% per annum are not unusual.

17
Keeping Your Accounts

Keeping financial accounts is the only way in which you can track the flow of funds into and out from your business. This is the most important element for all businesses. If you have lost control of your cash then you have probably lost control of your business. There is an old adage associated with financial accounts – 'cash is king' – ignore this at your peril.

WHY YOU NEED TO KEEP ACCOUNTS

Most businesses maintain some sort of accounting record, at the very least using a basic cash accounting system. Monitoring cash is very important to the day-to-day control of your business but it will not reveal any profits or losses that you are making.

Come the time for your annual accounts to be prepared, it will be too late to take any action. The trading performance is historic, the losses have been made and you cannot do a thing about it. The losses will have soaked up cash resources and, unless you have an extremely good action plan to improve your performance, you are unlikely to be able to gain outside funding.

This is a scenario that is repeated time and time again in all types of businesses. It is not only small firms that fail due to a lack of cash. Even large publicly quoted companies have failed for the same reason. If only business owners had taken the initiative and prepared even the most basic of accounts they could have recognised a potential problem before it occurred.

Keeping control of your business

Unfortunately many business owners go out of their way to avoid the preparation of financial accounts. It is difficult to establish the reasons for this, but the common theme seems to be that they are considered to be irrelevant to maintaining control. This is a grave and fundamental mistake. Control over your finances is a primary business function that you cannot afford to ignore. As part of that control, the accounts that you prepare will be a key indicator as to how your business is performing.

The accounts that you compile do not have to meet the exacting standards of the accountancy profession. They need only be used as a tool as part of your overall management control system. There is absolutely no reason why you cannot compile basic accounts for your own business.

> **TIP**
>
> Always remember it is your business – it is up to you to monitor your own financial performance.

I am not suggesting you can dispense with the services of an accountant. What I am suggesting is that you should use the specialist knowledge of your accountant for expert advice and to finalise your annual accounts. Unless you can afford to pay them for day-to-day involvement in your business they are of no relevance to the daily financial control of your business.

Statutory obligations

The keeping of adequate accounting records is usually necessary to comply with legislation. Each year many people fall foul of the Inland Revenue and HM Customs and Excise for failing to keep the proper records. Although, with the exception of a limited company, there is no legislation to force you to keep accounts, you could be in trouble if your business fails and you are declared bankrupt. This applies to any and every business.

A limited liability company must comply with the provisions of Section 221 of the Companies Act relating to a company's records. As a sole trader or as a partner in a partnership, if you are made bankrupt you could still be charged with failing to keep proper accounting records under section 361 of the Insolvency Act.

The penalties in both cases can be severe. The ultimate sanction for either of these offences is a prison sentence of up to seven years, an unlimited fine, or both.

> **TIP**
>
> These are not theoretical penalties – people do go to prison each year for failing to keep proper accounting records for their business.

If you operate as a limited company you are also required to lodge a copy of your accounts at Companies House. Bearing in mind the sensitive nature of accounting information, you will need the assistance of your accountant to ensure that only the very bare essentials are disclosed.

The different types of accounts

There are four different types of accounts:

◆ projected
◆ management
◆ annual
◆ audited.

The preparation of financial forecasts, or projected accounts, was covered in Chapter 13. In general most business owners have no problem with preparing projections for their business. Specialist business packs are available from the high street banks that contain specific projection forms for completion. The layout, styling and headings are relatively easy to understand.

Management accounts are accounts that enable you to manage your business. In most businesses, however, this form of accounts is totally ignored despite it being most important. It is this form of accounts that is of the most value to your business because these accounts will reveal whether you are making a profit or trading at a loss.

Management accounts are usually prepared on a monthly basis and are then compared with the projected accounts to assess ongoing performance. These accounts are important as they enable you to monitor your performance and to take early corrective action if necessary.

The third form of accounts is the annual accounts. These will normally be completed at your year-end by your accountant. These accounts are just as important to your business as the management accounts, but for different reasons. The annual accounts enable you to take the specialist advice of your accountant – for example, in order to minimise your tax liability.

TIP

There are exemptions available for completing audited accounts depending on the amount of turnover or sales you have made in the financial year.

Your accountant will also ensure that you comply with all relevant legislation concerning your accounting records and returns, especially if you operate as a limited liability company. Depending upon the size and type of your business you may be able to avoid compiling audited accounts.

If you are a limited company with turnover above a defined level then your accounts must be audited by a registered auditor. This means that the auditor will require a greater depth of knowledge of all your transactions. They will check and verify your documentation to make sure that the accounts are correctly prepared.

All of these forms of accounts are compiled using the same format. Each of these will involve:

◆ a balance sheet
◆ a profit and loss account.

BALANCE SHEET

The balance sheet will show the financial position of your business at a defined date. It is, therefore, merely a snap-shot of your business. The actual figures listed will have fluctuated throughout the year as your business makes sales and purchases. The individual components of the balance sheet will come under three headings:

◆ assets
◆ liabilities
◆ capital.

The first two headings will have a number of sub-headings relating to the individual asset and liability accounts that are in your books. The final heading, capital, will vary depending on what type of business you have. In simple terms at this stage these can be as follows:

◆ **Sole trader** – owner's capital account
◆ **Partnership** – partner's capital accounts (individually itemised)
◆ **Limited Company** – share capital.

How is it compiled?

The balance sheet is compiled from the asset and liability figures taken from your trial balance. These figures are placed in a logical format in order to arrive at the net worth, or surplus resources, of your business. In an ideal world, the figure should always be positive. This means that you have a surplus of assets over liabilities and, if the business were to fail, you would be able to pay off all of your creditors.

If the figure is negative this means that your liabilities exceed your assets. Without an injection of cash into the business, preferably from your own resources, the business would be unable to meet its debts as they become payable. If you encounter this situation you must seek the immediate advice of your accountant. Even if you operate as a limited company you could still incur personal liability under certain circumstances if you continue to trade.

Is it an accurate value of the business?

The plain and simple answer is no. The balance sheet is compiled using the 'book' value of assets. For example, if you purchase a motor vehicle the actual cost is entered in the books. Over time this may be reduced by depreciation. This will still not represent the actual resale value of the vehicle should it become necessary to sell it. It could recover more, or less, than the defined 'book' value.

> **TIP**
>
> If your business does fail you need to be aware that all of your assets may have a book value but they are only worth what people will actually pay for them – this could be substantially less than you think.

As a further example, consider the accounts of your debtors, the people who owe you money for goods or services that you have provided. When you compile your balance sheet you are making the assumption that all your debtors will meet their obligations. It is possible that some of them may fail to pay their debt. This will, of course, affect the value of your business as well.

THE PROFIT AND LOSS ACCOUNT

The profit and loss account is probably the most important account for all businesses. Unless you are making a profit there is little point in being in business.

What will it show?

The profit and loss account covers all of your trading activity for the accounting period in question, usually 12 months. This period may vary, however, usually in the first year of trading, not only to take account of the requirements of the Inland Revenue but also to make your tax return easier to prepare.

The profit and loss account will summarise your sales income, or turnover, and itemise the actual cost of those sales. This will lead to the calculation of your gross profit. Your other overhead expenses will then be deducted to arrive at a net profit figure. The profit and loss account will then show how that profit has been distributed using an appropriation account.

Where do the figures come from?

As with all the other figures in your financial accounts the profit and loss figures will come from your trial balance. The one exception will be the figure for closing stock. The only way that this figure can be accurately obtained is by undertaking a physical stock check, or stock-take, of all the unsold goods. A value can then be placed on them, based on the cost price or the net realisable value, whichever is lower.

Once you have this information you can then calculate the actual cost of goods sold:

Opening stock plus purchases less your closing stock = cost of goods sold

This method will have given you the relevant information regarding your stock value, but at this stage no double entries have been made in the books.

COMPARING ACTUAL PERFORMANCE WITH YOUR FORECASTS

To enable you to run your business efficiently you must review your actual trading results against your original forecasts. Many businesses totally ignore this. Financial forecasts are put together, the business plan is written and used to raise finance, and then the forecasts along with the business plan are put in a drawer and forgotten.

This is a recipe for disaster. Unless you carefully monitor your performance on a regular basis you run the risk of running out of cash. Once that happens it can be difficult to raise more finance because all you have demonstrated to the potential funder is that you have failed to keep control of your business.

Relating actual performance to targets

On a monthly basis at least you should take some time to analyse your financial performance for that month. This means that you must categorise and total up all your income and expenditure and compare the actual figures to your forecasted target figures. Ideally, this should be done on a rolling cumulative basis allowing comparison with not only the monthly figures but also the cumulative figures to date.

Comparing your actual performance against your forecasted figures in this way will enable you to gain a greater understanding of exactly how your business is performing over time. It may well be that one month's figures could be distorted in some way, possibly by a large amount of capital expenditure being deferred for payment one month later than anticipated. This sort of distortion in the figures will have a marked effect in both the forecasted month for the expenditure and the actual month in which it was incurred.

> **TIP**
>
> Compare your figures on a cumulative basis and you should even out any distortion in the monthly figures.

Taking remedial action

Comparing your figures on a monthly and cumulative basis will also enable you to take corrective action. If you are over budget you can trim down future expenditure and, if you are within budget, you can either take the savings or spend more in later months. The critical point, however, is that by compiling management accounts you do at least give yourself a choice.

This is an important point to remember. Maintaining tight control over your finances means that you increase the options available to you. If you constantly monitor your income and expenditure you can adjust your budgets or your spending throughout the year. On the other hand, if you maintain little or no control over your ongoing finances then you have no options at all. At the end of the year when the final accounts are prepared it is too late to do anything if you have made a loss.

COMPUTERISING YOUR ACCOUNTS

Whatever business you run, you really should have a full computer system and printer to organise your business. There can be no excuses whatsoever for not having a computer, given the substantial reductions in price over the years. It is no longer necessary to pay thousands of pounds for a system.

A computer-based accounting system will offer substantial benefits in the way in which you run your business. These will include:

◆ less time spent 'doing the books'
◆ accurate and up-to-date management information
◆ faster production of annual accounts
◆ cost savings on book-keeping and accountancy charges.

TIP

It is not just the financial side of your business that will benefit from a computer – you can also use it to organise all of your correspondence, marketing materials, and customer databases, to name just a few functions.

The use of such an accountancy system will reduce the more mundane tasks involved in keeping your own accounts. Your existing records must, however, be kept adequately. If you have an inadequate system now, computerising your accounts will not solve the problem.

THE BENEFITS OF COMPUTERISING YOUR ACCOUNTS

Having a computerised accounting system will save you time and, hopefully, also money. Anyway that you can make cost efficient savings in your business should be welcomed.

You may not, for example, need to employ the services of a book-keeper. Instead, you will need a member of staff who can use the software program. You will no longer need to keep vast amounts of paper-based records. All of your finances can be organised in the computer's memory. With a few simple actions you should be able to gain information on all your customers' accounts, complete with an analysis of their payment records. In essence, a computer-based accountancy system will give you greater control.

Management reports

All of the management accounts discussed previously should be available. Within minutes you should be able to see exactly how your business has performed. This can be analysed on a daily, weekly, monthly or annual basis or any other time period that you choose.

The balance sheet and profit and loss accounts are updated with each entry that you make. You can see at a glance how you are doing in terms of the key indicators of profitability and liquidity. You can access these reports at any time and, more importantly, take speedy action if your finances are not going as planned.

You could also analyse your debtors and creditors with immediate reports on:

TIP

The computer has all the information needed to compile your management accounts – all you have to do is ask for it.

◆ who owes you money
◆ how long they are taking to pay you
◆ who you owe money to
◆ how long their invoices have been outstanding.

All this sort of information is not readily available with a paper-based system. Potentially, with a paper-based accounting system it could take you several hours to prepare this sort of analysis.

Forecasting

This is another area in which a computer-based accounting system really comes into its own. It will enable you to prepare all of the forecasts and financial statements that we have previously considered:

◆ cash flow forecasts
◆ balance sheet
◆ profit and loss account.

It will be relatively simple for you to base your forecasts on historic performance. You can also ask the computer 'what if' type questions. Once you have prepared the basic forecasts you could, for example, apply a set increase in sales to see what the results would be. Or, you could apply a decrease in sales, or an increase in costs, or both, to see how this would affect your business.

These sorts of calculations could take you hours to undertake using a manual system. In addition to the above, you can undertake a detailed analysis of your costs within minutes, comparing any number of combinations of figures using the computer. Once again, these sorts of benefits offer you substantially more control over a paper-based system.

What choice of software do I have?

The choice of software that you make will depend on a number of factors including:

◆ the type of computer hardware that you have
◆ the size of your business
◆ whether you have, or envisage having, any employees
◆ whether you are, or will be at some stage, registered for VAT.

TIP

The important point to consider is that you will be using this software, hopefully, for a long time and it must therefore serve its purpose for the foreseeable future.

The real question you need to ask is exactly what it is that you want from the software. You need to decide what functions are essential, what would be nice to have if possible, and perhaps even what you do not need at all.

There are software packages available from a wide number of software houses. Some of the most common are:

◆ Sage
◆ TAS Books
◆ Pegasus
◆ Intuit.

The choice that you make must be the one that is the most appropriate for your business. Most of these software providers produce a range of software based on the size of the business that will be utilising it. Sage at present have a number of accounting packages from the most basic, 'Instant Accounting' up to the most comprehensive, 'Sovereign'.

One of the most important considerations to remember when making your choice is that the software must be capable of growing with your business. Most businesses start out small and then grow over a period of time. It would be pointless to purchase a software solution that did not offer the same facility. Once you have made your choice, and entered all of the opening information, you will not want to use that system for a few years only to find that it becomes obsolete and you have to start again. Make sure that the chosen package allows for upgrades or the addition of further features without you having to enter all of your data again.

You may decide that you need to purchase the most complex software solution in order to guard against obsolescence. Nothing wrong with that but, one word of warning, it will also probably be the most difficult to use.

> **TIP**
>
> It is better to start with a simple package which you can then upgrade as and when you need to.

Ensuring compatibility

This really is part of the decision-making process. Apart from ensuring that the software will follow you as you grow, it is better to purchase software that is compatible with any used by your accountant. Without this compatibility you may as well be speaking different languages.

Your accountant can also probably advise you on the most suitable software for your business. They will hopefully already have experience with similar-sized businesses as yours and will already have helped others with any problems. You should never be in too much of a hurry to choose your software. Make the right decision at the outset and you could well save a lot of time and trouble later.

Timing the transition

This aspect is extremely important if previously you have used a manual accounting system and you are now going to computerise your accounts. You will need to arrange a cut-off date for the manual system after which you will use the new computerised system. This is a process you should not rush. Make sure you understand how your chosen software package works before you attempt to enter any data. A few errors at the outset could well take you a long time to solve later.

You must also make sure that your final manual records balance. The computer cannot later help you solve errors if the initial opening balances were incorrect. You will, for example, need to draw up a final manual balance sheet and profit and loss account that will identify and provide the opening balances for the computerised version of your accounts. Planning the transition is just as important as actually taking the decision to computerise your accounts and deciding on which software package to use.

TIP
As with all elements of your accounts, without an accurate and solid foundation you may end up with computerised accounts that can never be accurate.

Getting help

You must be under no illusions. Computerising your accounts is far from an easy process. Many of the business support organisations offer subsidised training in some of the popular computer software packages and, wherever possible, you would be advised to gain as much help as you can.

You may also find that the software producers themselves offer specific training in their products, Sage being a prime example. It is well worth checking around before you purchase the software to see what support you can obtain. Do not rely on any help-line offered by the software producer. They are only there to offer technical support. They cannot, and indeed will not, provide free support if you are trying to solve any problems caused by entering data in the wrong place.

It cannot be emphasised too strongly that you must know exactly how the software works before you start to use it. In some cases, especially with a complicated original manual-based system, it is well worth enlisting the help of either a professional or the software supplier themselves to manage the transition for you.

TIP

Check with your local Business Link to see if they offer any form of training on using your chosen software package.

18

Looking at Franchising Options

The term 'franchisor' refers to the seller of the franchise and 'franchisee' refers to the purchaser of the franchise. A franchise is a business relationship between the franchisor, who has a tried and tested business concept, and yourself who purchases the right to operate a branded business. It will involve a capital investment plus ongoing royalty or management fees based either on sales turnover or as a mark-up on goods supplied for resale by the franchisor.

The franchisor will provide initial training in all aspects of the franchise in order to ensure that you are equipped to run the franchise successfully. The franchisor will also provide ongoing assistance and support to you in all aspects of the franchise operation.

THE ADVANTAGES AND DISADVANTAGES OF A FRANCHISE

There are obvious advantages in buying a franchise, the most important being that you will be purchasing a tried and tested business concept. It may not be cheaper than starting your own business in the same sort of market but it does bring with it a recognised brand image. It is estimated that whilst only one in five new-start businesses will still be trading after five years, some 90% of franchise operations will have succeeded.

> **TIP**
>
> Buying a franchise is not a recipe for business success – you will still need to work extremely hard.

The benefits

There are numerous benefits in buying a franchise some of which are:

◆ You will have the opportunity to purchase a business concept that has already been tried and tested in the market.

◆ The risks of setting up a franchised business are substantially reduced when compared to establishing a new business in the same market.

◆ A franchise will provide a brand image that the public will recognise.

◆ Business premises will all comply with an established interior and exterior design to assist with brand promotion.

◆ Specifications for the equipment required by the franchise will be clearly identified from the outset.

◆ Publicity and ongoing marketing can be arranged by the franchisor as part of the contractual agreement.

◆ Comprehensive training in all aspects of running the business will be given to you by the franchisor, both initially and on an ongoing basis as methods are improved.

◆ The 'operations manual' received as part of the franchise will give standardised procedures for accounting, sales, and stock control.

◆ The franchisor may be able to provide you with better terms for the centralised bulk purchase of raw materials or goods used by the franchise.

◆ As the franchisee, you should benefit from the franchisor's ongoing research and development undertaken to improve the franchised product or service.

◆ Networking with other franchisees will provide both you and the franchisor with opportunities for review and improvement of the operating procedures.

◆ The franchise should have a clearly defined geographical area within which the rights of the franchise are protected from other franchises from the same franchisor.

The final advantage of purchasing a franchise, as opposed to starting your own business, relates to raising funding for the venture. Gaining finance to purchase a franchise is generally easier than gaining finance to start a new business. The reason for this is that the franchisor will be better able to provide estimates of the likely sales and costs, thereby giving a more accurate prediction of profit levels.

Most of the high street banks have specialist franchise sections that monitor the ongoing progress of their franchise customers. In this way they build up a picture of the success, or otherwise, of a franchise. Whilst they will not pass on an opinion as to ongoing viability, they will obviously be more prepared to finance a franchise that has a successful history.

Under some circumstances the franchisor may be able to offer assistance with funding. A well-established franchisor will often make arrangements with a particular bank to fund the purchase of a franchise. You, as franchisee, will still have responsibility for the loan, but the involvement of the franchisor may increase the likelihood that the loan will be granted.

If you are having difficulty in obtaining finance for the purchase of a franchise you should perhaps be looking at it more carefully.

The disadvantages

As with all business ventures there are some disadvantages to buying a franchise. Being a franchisee means that you are buying a total business concept and there is subsequently no room for individuality in terms of the product or service offered. The franchisor will demand that all aspects of the business are operated exactly as set out in the 'operations manual' with uniform standards for appearance and packaging of the goods or services.

Many prospective franchisees feel that they can improve on the way that things are done. That may well be the case but, unless the franchisor agrees, you will be forced to conduct your business exactly as they tell you.

Once a franchise has been purchased it can be difficult to dispose of as there are often limitations placed on any re-sale. The franchisor will, more than likely, want to approve the potential purchaser, and they will probably want some control over the sale price.

> **TIP**
>
> Remember that whilst you may have exclusive territorial rights there is, of course, nothing to stop customers from obtaining the same goods or services from another franchisee in a neighbouring territory.

It can also be extremely difficult to enforce exclusive territory rights. When you purchase a franchise, the franchisor will usually undertake not to sell another franchise within a defined geographical area.

Disputes over the royalty fee or management charge that is usually based on sales turnover or profits are not uncommon. As part of the contractual agreement the franchisor will normally undertake centralised marketing campaigns, for if these are not undertaken it will undoubtedly have an impact on sales. By the same token, it could be that the franchisor undertakes marketing campaigns that have little benefit for a particular franchisee in, say, a remote location.

Disputes over the royalty fee based on sales turnover can arise over special promotions. With the franchisor's income from you depending on volume of turnover they may not be concerned with your overall profitability. Whilst this is a rather short-sighted attitude it is possible for the franchisor to insist upon price cuts or special offers that will increase turnover, and therefore their royalty fee, at the expense of your profitability.

As well as the royalty fee you may be forced, under the terms of the franchise, to buy goods and services only from the franchisor. Apart from the fact that these could be at disadvantaged prices it should be remembered that the franchisor will also normally have control over the selling price. This effectively gives the franchisor the right to control overall profit margins.

The final disadvantage is the possibility that the franchisor may fail, leaving you with a business that may not be viable in isolation. It should be remembered that the franchisor will place all manner of controls and obligations on you.

> **TIP**
>
> It is unlikely that you will be able to control the actions of the franchisor and if they receive any bad publicity this will affect the whole brand or image of the franchise.

DIFFERENT TYPES OF FRANCHISE

Franchising opportunities are available for all sorts of businesses in all manner of markets and provided the original concept can be replicated it may be suitable to be franchised. In order to assess whether a business is suitable for a potential franchise there are a number of criteria that you will need to consider:

- The original business concept must have been tried and tested and proved to be a success.
- The franchise should be capable of a distinct brand image in addition to having standardised systems and methods.
- The systems and methods must be capable of being clearly defined within an operations manual so as to transfer this knowledge to you.
- Operation of the franchise must provide you with sufficient profitability to reward you for the original investment and ongoing work.
- The franchise also needs to generate sufficient income for the franchisor in terms of the sale of the original business concept and the ongoing income from management fees or royalties.

Characteristics of a franchise

When deciding whether a business is capable of being operated as a franchise it is obviously necessary for you to consider the characteristics of the business. In some ways it is easier to consider the potential by looking at the characteristics that could render a business unsuitable for franchising. These could include:

◆ products that have a very short life span in the market
◆ businesses with minimal profitability
◆ services that require considerable training to reach the required skill level
◆ businesses with repeat business based on loyalty to an individual rather than a product or service
◆ businesses that are specific to one geographical area.

In summary, there are no real boundaries to franchising most business concepts provided they meet the basic criteria for a franchise. Franchising can be an excellent opportunity for you to run your own business using an original successful concept with proven marketing and operating methods.

> **TIP**
>
> A successful franchise is really a partnership between you, as the franchisee, and the franchisor, who will provide ongoing support behind the scenes.

WHAT WILL THE FRANCHISE OFFER?

When selecting a franchise you need to be clear about exactly what it is you are being offered and what form of franchise it is. There are three types of franchise:

◆ **Job franchise** – effectively you are purchasing a job for yourself. The capital investment required will usually range from £5,000 up to £20,000 and these franchises take the form of single-person businesses. Examples include mobile car mechanics and domestic carpet or fabric cleaners.

◆ **Business franchise** – these involve the purchase of a complete business that will require additional staff over and above your own involvement. Prices for this type of franchise range from £20,000 to £100,000. Examples include fast food operations and printing shops.

◆ **Investment franchise** – at the top of the scale and usually involving a substantial investment in excess of £100,000 with some costing as much as £1m. As would be expected, there are few franchises in this price range. Examples include hotels and restaurants. The vast majority of the franchise investment cost in these cases will be for the property and equipment required.

From the above you will see that it is easy to establish exactly what type of franchise you are being offered. What is sometimes more difficult to establish is exactly what you are being offered as part of the deal. Taking the case of a mobile mechanic, does the franchise fee include a customised vehicle and all equipment? Understanding what you get for your money is extremely important.

Being on your guard

You need to be aware that some so-called franchisors are not actually offering a franchise at all. As with all aspects of business, there are potential fraudsters in the market and you need to be on your guard. Before you make any initial decisions on a prospective franchise you must always obtain references. You should also contact the British Franchise Association to establish whether the franchise you are considering are members. If they are not then you need to ask why not and whether they intend applying in due course. The decision will, of course, rest with you but wide research is required before you make a final choice.

> **TIP**
>
> Make sure that you talk to your bank before making a selection – they have specialists who deal with franchising and they can offer specific help and guidance.

THE COST OF THE FRANCHISE

The amount of the initial cost will depend on two factors – whether the franchise fee is solely for the business concept or whether it also includes all of the equipment necessary to trade. In the majority of cases the up-front fee will represent 10% of the total start-up costs. This fee will only relate to the sale by the franchisor of the business concept. It still leaves you to finance the required premises and equipment.

This means that the total start-up costs for each franchise will vary from franchise to franchise depending on location. In some of the more complex franchise deals the franchisor will acquire and equip the property for a franchisee. However, there may still be a difference in the total cost of the franchise relating to the cost of the property.

The franchisor may also opt for a small fee initially but a larger percentage as an ongoing royalty. Conversely, there may be a large up-front fee and reduced ongoing costs. It will depend on how the franchisor wishes to recoup his costs. Some will reduce the initial financial start-up burden on the basis that their costs, together with a profit, will be paid over time by way of the royalty payments.

> **TIP**
>
> Make sure that you understand the full costs of the franchise before you sign anything – it is too late to change your mind once you have signed the contract.

Ongoing costs

There are a number of different terms for the ongoing costs:
◆ management fees
◆ service charges
◆ royalties.

There are also two main methods of calculation, either based upon a percentage of turnover or a fixed monthly fee. In some cases, a minimum level of fee is also imposed. The most common method of calculation is on a percentage of turnover and you can expect to pay between 5% and 10%.

This is regarded as the fairest method of charging. It means that you know exactly what you will have to pay and it can be calculated relatively easily. From the franchisor's point of view it means that they will also benefit from the growth in your business.

The important consideration for ongoing fees is to satisfy yourself that they are fair and that you cannot be exploited by the franchisor. These fees are to pay for the ongoing assistance of the franchisor and they must relate clearly to the perceived value of that assistance.

What do I get for my money?

What you will get for your money will depend upon the individual franchise package. Remember that you are also buying a business concept and image and therefore you will also be paying for intangible goodwill. In the most basic franchise package there will be two key elements:

◆ The brand name and image – a licence to trade under the name of the franchisor in a specified location and for a determinate period.
◆ Practical training together with an 'operations manual' – full training in how to conduct the business. The 'operations manual' will outline the procedures and methods to be followed in running the franchise.

The franchise package should include the grant of a licence by the franchisor to you to use the brand name and image in your own business. This will be for a limited period of time and the terms and conditions of renewal should be clearly defined. It must also contain exclusive territorial rights with an undertaking by the franchisor not to sell a further franchise within a defined area.

Also included will be details of the products or services to be sold and whether or not they must be purchased from the franchisor. If the franchisor is a manufacturer, with you operating a retail outlet, there can be no doubt that the franchisor will only allow the sale of their own goods. Even if the franchisor themselves are retailers it is likely they will insist upon being your only supplier. This could be to your advantage, as the franchisor may have negotiated substantial discounts with their own suppliers for bulk purchases that should, at least in part, be passed on to you.

For a franchise in a service industry, the 'operations manual' will form the most valuable asset of the franchise package. It will contain, in fine detail, the procedures and methods to be adopted in running the business. It will be provided to you as part of your initial training and should equip you with all the required skills to operate the franchise. It will also outline the financial and other reporting requirements for the management information system operated by the franchisor.

> **TIP**
>
> When you are considering buying a franchise the most important consideration is to satisfy yourself that you will receive value for money and ongoing assistance to help you succeed.

19

Buying an Existing Business

Businesses are bought and sold for a variety of reasons just like any other commodity. There are, unfortunately, a number of severe problems involved in buying an existing business and it is essential that you have professional assistance from the outset. At the very least you will require a competent commercial lawyer together with an accountant who has experience in this field.

TIP

You can obtain details of businesses for sale from a number of sources including estate agents, trade magazines and the business pages of the quality newspapers.

In view of the complexities involved in buying an existing business I will not attempt to try to explain the process. What I will do is give you some idea of the problems that may be encountered. I will also make the assumption that you have identified a potential business to purchase.

UNDERTAKING A PERSONAL INSPECTION OF THE BUSINESS

Having identified a suitable potential business to purchase you will need to make a significant number of visits. These should be conducted at different times, on different days, to gain an overall feel of how the business operates. They will also give you a chance to meet any staff and assess how well they work.

To a large extent the format of the visits that you make will vary from business to business. If, for example, you are considering the purchase of a retail shop you will not actually need to go inside on all visits. Some can be done by purely sitting outside to measure the number of customers who enter.

Whenever you do visit you must be alert and take in all that is going on around you. Do not spend all your time talking to the owner or the staff. This will merely distract you from the real purpose of your visits which is to establish just how active the business is. Some of the things that you should be looking for include:

- Is there a regular flow of customers?
- Is the layout of the business suitable?
- How tidy is the business?
- Does the telephone ring often?
- Are the staff courteous and efficient?
- Are all of the staff kept busy?
- What does the condition of the stock look like?

VALUING THE BUSINESS

This is probably the most difficult aspect for you to consider. Obviously, the vendor will want as high a price as possible while you will want to pay as little as you can. There will probably be a number of components making up the final price. The first thing that you will need to do is establish exactly what those components will be. To do that you will require up-to-date audited accounts. Let us take a theoretical example.

Balance Sheet of XYZ Engineering Ltd

Fixed Assets

Land and buildings	£100,000
Plant and machinery	£30,000
Tools and equipment	£15,000
Motor vehicles	£30,000
	£175,000

Current Assets

Trade debtors	£25,000
Raw materials	£10,000
Finished goods	£20,000
Cash at bank	£5,000
	£60,000

Total Assets   **£235,000**

Current Liabilities

Trade creditors	£15,000
Other creditors	£10,000
Hire purchase	£5,000
Bank loan	£5,000
	£35,000

Long-Term Liabilities

Hire purchase	£15,000
Bank loan	£35,000
	£50,000

Net Assets   **£150,000**

Represented by:

Share Capital	£50,000
Profit and Loss Account	£100,000
	£150,000

On the face of it, this business is worth £150,000 – or is it? Remember these figures are all 'book' valuations. Further examination will be required to confirm the 'book' valuations as realistic. Let us break down the individual components and examine the reasons for possible distortion.

Fixed Assets

The fixed assets will more than likely have been valued at the original cost price less any depreciation that has been allocated. Their true value may, however, be substantially different. For example:

◆ **Land and buildings** – If the property was purchased some time ago it may have increased in value. By the same token, if it was purchased recently and property prices have since fallen, the true value may be less. The only way to establish the correct price is to have the property valued by a professional.

◆ **Plant and machinery** – The 'book' value will bear no relation to the 'true' value because resale prices are likely to be substantially less. Within the existing business, however, their value is pure conjecture. You will need to consider the condition of the items involved and whether the depreciation is realistic.

◆ **Tools and equipment** – The valuation of small items such as these will prove to be extremely difficult. It could actually be virtually impossible to identify all of the individual items involved.

◆ **Motor vehicles** – Just as with the plant and machinery, the 'true' valuation is likely to differ from the 'book' valuation. With a small number of vehicles, as in this case, it should be relatively simple to gain a valuation from a motoring organisation. With a large number of vehicles the situation is more complicated. It is probable that a number of the vehicles involved will be 'on the road' and away from the business premises.

Current assets

With all of these assets being 'liquid', the actual figures involved are likely to be substantially different. Unlike the fixed assets, which remain relatively unchanged over short periods, the current assets will change on a daily basis. For this reason, they cannot be accurately

TIP

Up-to-date accounts do not mean the last set of accounts prepared. The balance sheet only provides a 'snap-shot' of the business and therefore the accounts should be no more than one month out of date.

valued until the business actually changes hands. Nevertheless, there are a number of pitfalls to catch the unwary:

◆ **Trade debtors** – Some of these could be potential bad debts if they have been outstanding for a long period of time. You will need to examine an 'aged' debtor list and probably exclude any debts that have been outstanding for longer than the business's normal terms of trade. For example, if the terms of trade are 30 days then you may wish to exclude those that are one month overdue for payment, i.e. ones that are 60 days old.

◆ **Raw materials** – These will have been valued at cost price but until they are actually turned into finished goods their value is probably minimal on a resale basis. It is also possible that some of the raw materials could be extremely old and unusable. It will depend on the way in which the stock is used. The only way that a 'true' figure can be obtained is by physically examining all the stock and comparing the price to the costs of replacement.

◆ **Finished goods** – The same criteria will apply to the finished goods as to the raw materials. Some of the stock could be damaged and unsaleable. An accurate value can only be achieved by actually examining and counting all the goods.

◆ **Cash at bank** – This is probably the easiest value to confirm. It is likely, however, that it will be excluded from the business valuation. There is little point in exchanging cash via the purchase price for cash in a bank account.

Liabilities
The current liabilities and the long-term liabilities can be considered together for the reason that in this instance, the hire purchase and bank loan

have been split purely for accounting purposes. On any given day both of these will show the same individual amount in the current liabilities section representing the amount that is due within the next 12 months.

◆ **Trade creditors** – These should be treated in the same way as trade debtors and will need to be examined for the length of time they have been outstanding. You also need to consider the fact that some of these trade creditors may not wish to grant you credit when you take over the business. Their relationship is with the existing owner and not you, who have yet to build a trade reputation. You will need to confirm the position before you agree to buy the business.

◆ **Other creditors** – Within this figure will be the amounts owed to the Inland Revenue for National Insurance and Income Tax. It will also include any amount due to HM Customs and Excise in respect of VAT. It is vitally important that you establish that any sums due have been paid on time.

◆ **Hire purchase** – Any amounts due in this respect will be secured on the assets that were purchased using the funds. You will need to examine the relevant agreements and ensure that all instalments have been paid to date. You cannot afford to run the risk of the assets being repossessed once you have bought the business.

◆ **Bank loan** – In the same way as with the hire purchase you will need to see the loan agreement form. For a loan of this amount it is likely that some form of security has been given and this will need to be investigated. If, for example, the existing owner has granted some form of personal security it is possible that the bank may require replacement security from you before the business can be sold.

Considering any 'goodwill' amount
It is likely that even if no amount is included within the balance sheet you will be faced with a request for a suitable sum to be paid for

'goodwill'. This is a difficult figure to establish because it is not represented by any tangible assets. It relates purely to an intangible asset that the vendor now wishes to try to value. It might include items such as:

◆ strong commercial reputation
◆ established brand names, trademarks, or copyrights
◆ future products that are reaching the end of their research and development.

TIP
Always remember that goodwill can disappear very easily. Where the business has been built on a personal reputation this may be lost as soon as the business is sold.

This is an area where extreme care is required. The existing owner will argue that they have built up the business to what it is now and they deserve some benefit. Unless there is a large retained sum in the profit and loss account you must remember, however, that they have already withdrawn their reward from operating the business.

MANAGING THE PURCHASE PROCESS

Hopefully, by this stage, you will have recognised the difficulties involved in valuing a business. Most of these problems can be resolved by a suitably qualified accountant. Before you can agree a final price, however, you must undertake a process known as 'due diligence'. Effectively, this process will investigate all aspects of the business and it will take some time to complete. This is where only a commercial lawyer can help you. They will ensure that the business has complied with all relevant legislation and that the records are complete and accurate. They can also assist you with:

◆ Drawing up a suitable contract of sale – with appropriate provisions to stop the vendor setting up a new business in competition. It may

also include some element of assistance
from the vendor in running the business
jointly for a limited period to ensure a
smooth hand-over.

◆ Compiling a schedule of all assets and
liabilities that are to be included in the deal
and the agreed valuation or details of how
they will be valued.

◆ Searching the registers at Companies House for details of all directors
of the business, the shareholders and any security that has been granted.

◆ Completing the necessary forms to register the transfer of the
business and the names of the new directors and shareholders with
Companies House.

◆ Investigating the property with the local planning authority – you
will need to ensure that no changes to the surrounding areas are
proposed that could adversely affect the business.

FINANCIAL CONSIDERATIONS

Unless you are able to afford to buy the business without borrowing
any money you will need to consider the financial implications on the
business. To illustrate this point it is easier to look at a specific
example. Consider the following hypothetical figures from a profit and
loss account:

Profit and Loss Account for XYZ Engineering Ltd

Sales		£500,000
Cost of sales	£300,000	
Gross Profit		£200,000
Overheads	£100,000	
Directors' remuneration	£75,000	
Net Profit		£25,000

Let us assume that the asking price for this business is £1m. In the absence of any borrowed money and adding back the existing directors' remuneration you can expect net profits, provided you achieve the same level of sales and costs remain the same, at about £100,000 per annum.

If you have had to raise finance to complete the purchase you will need to pay for this finance from the existing profits. As an example, the asking price remains £1m but this time this has been financed by:

◆ your own capital injection – £100,000
◆ venture capital – £500,000
◆ bank loan – £400,000.

Your own capital

Apart from the opportunity cost of not investing your money in, for example, stocks and shares or a building society, your own investment will not cost you anything. The return that you gain should, of course, come from the profits that the business makes. This will, however, come to you only if you make a profit.

Venture capital

The only way that you could gain any bank funding would be if a venture capitalist invested in the business by way of shares. This funding is expensive, however, and the agreed terms in this case are for a 20% return per annum. In addition, the shares are to be bought back by you over a ten-year period.

In this case the costs in the first year will amount to £100,000 interest and capital repayments of £50,000 – a total cost of £150,000.

Bank loan

The bank loan has been agreed over a ten-year period with interest fixed at 10% for the entire term of the loan. The total costs in the first year will therefore be interest of approximately £40,000 together with capital repayments of £40,000 – a total cost of £80,000.

The effect on profitability

It should be obvious that the effects on profitability are severe. With a net profit, before your own remuneration and any finance costs, of £100,000, the business will now make a substantial loss as follows:

Net profit		£100,000
Venture capital costs	£150,000	
Bank repayments	£80,000	
		£230,000
Net loss		(£130,000)

Clearly this would not be an attractive proposition and indeed, it is unlikely that you would be able to gain such funding on this basis. There are simply inadequate profits to ensure repayment. It has, however, demonstrated the difference that can be made to the profitability of a business when the purchase is funded by outside borrowing. This aspect should feature highly on your list of things to consider when buying an existing business.

> **TIP**
>
> Carefully evaluate how the existing costs of the business will change once it has been taken over. Additional costs could make the purchase financially unviable.

20

Maintaining Quality Standards

Most small businesses ignore the issue of quality. This is very unfortunate because in most cases it could provide an extra competitive advantage. If you think about it rationally most small businesses cannot compete with larger businesses who may have economies of scale, for example bulk purchasing discounts. What they can do, however, is offer a better quality of service.

Put yourself in the shoes of your customers. If they receive a shoddy service or their complaints go unheeded are they likely to use your business again? Many businesses do not use complaints constructively. If you have a recognised complaints procedure, and your customers know how to use it, it can actually work to your advantage. If you know something is wrong you can do something about it.

WHAT EXACTLY IS QUALITY?

The concept of quality is generally misunderstood. Many businesses consider that the introduction of quality management will place an added cost burden on their business. Actually quite the reverse is true. Substantial savings can be made by removing the causes of any problems that lead to complaints. Say, for example, you operate a manufacturing business. Inevitably there will be some wastage in the raw materials that you use. By implementing a quality management programme to reduce that wastage you will reduce your costs of production, leading to a rise in profits.

Whatever your type of business, if you operate to the highest possible standards, it can only enhance your reputation. You do not need to have a 'manual' to operate a quality system. What you do need is a positive attitude. We have already established that if you are to succeed you must offer something that your customer wants. Almost certainly what they will want is to be assured that your products will be fit for their purpose. This means that the product must be of a high standard and logically this means of good quality.

Take as an example the clothing industry. If you want to purchase a quality garment you will probably not go to a high street chain that sells mass-produced items. You will, instead, visit a small boutique or tailor that can make a garment specifically for you. Almost certainly you will pay a higher price, but the quality is what matters, not the cost.

> **TIP**
>
> Do not confuse quality with class. If you purchase a car, whether it be a Rolls Royce or a Ford, you still expect a quality product that is fit for its purpose – in this case getting you from one place to another.

LINKING QUALITY TO YOUR OBJECTIVES

Your quality management must be linked to your overall business objectives. In a similar way, once your objectives have been reached you will need to set new objectives. Some of your existing objectives may already be linked to quality. If you have a staff training programme this can only lead to a better standard of service. Some common examples of objectives linked to quality are:

◆ reduce product returns
◆ increase customer satisfaction
◆ invest in new technology
◆ undertake market research
◆ reduce the costs of production.

When you set your quality objectives make sure that they meet the SMART criteria outlined in Chapter 3.

LINKING QUALITY TO COMPETITIVE ADVANTAGE

A quality management programme can also give you a competitive advantage. With any small business, the relationship between the owner and their customers is significantly closer than for larger businesses. In effect, a small business is seen as offering a personal service whereas larger businesses are often seen as impersonal.

By the same token a small business will have substantially less customers than a larger business. This means that every customer is much more important to the small business. By far the cheapest means of gaining business is from satisfied customers who come back. They are also likely to recommend you to their friends. This can, of course, also work in reverse. We will look at dealing with complaints from dissatisfied customers a little later in this chapter.

> **TIP**
>
> Word of mouth can be very powerful and people that are dissatisfied can be very vocal in complaining about you to everyone – except you.

Earlier in this book I cautioned against trying to compete solely on price. If this is your only competitive advantage it could be eroded if your customers consider that your products are inferior in quality. It is far preferable to provide some type of added value that your customers can recognise. This could take many forms, for example:

◆ free delivery
◆ free maintenance for a limited period
◆ free fitting of appliances
◆ free telephone support.

While offered as 'free', all of these options can be costed and included in your actual price. The main point is that the customer recognises the benefit and is consequently prepared to pay a little extra for the quality of service offered.

As an example, when it is time to change my car I have used the same car dealership for many years. I also use the same dealer for all the maintenance and servicing required. The reason for this can be summed up in one word – quality. The vehicles I have purchased from them have been absolutely spotless inside and out. That even includes the engine compartment, which is rigorously steam-cleaned. When a regular service is due they telephone me to arrange a convenient date. On that day they come and collect my vehicle, leave a replacement for me to use and then return my vehicle when the work is completed.

There is no doubt that I could probably save money by going somewhere else but this would involve added inconvenience. I am prepared to pay a little extra for what I consider to be a good quality of service.

DEALING WITH COMPLAINTS

Some businesses loathe receiving complaints and, quite frankly, have a very poor attitude when dealing with them. You must always view a complaint as an opportunity. You are being told about something that a customer considers is wrong. Far better that they tell you and give you an opportunity to do something about it than keep quiet and not use your business again.

You do, of course, have to consider in the first place whether a complaint is justified or not. If you are in a service-based business you may find that some customers will only complain when you have finished the work, sent the invoice, and are now chasing them for late payment. Under these circumstances you would probably not wish to work with that customer again in any event.

Where a complaint is justified then you must take steps to rectify the situation. Never be afraid to offer some form of recompense if, for example, the complaint does not relate to the quality of your product, but where events outside of your control have caused the problem. After all, as the business owner you should have ensured that you had total control over the situation.

The overriding principle when dealing with complaints is to ensure that you satisfy the customer so that they will continue to use your business. A few points in this respect:

◆ Always listen to the complaint carefully without interruption.
◆ Never attempt to argue the point until you have heard all that the customer has to say.
◆ Show sympathy towards what has happened.
◆ Take notes about what they say and ask questions of clarification after they have finished outlining the problem.
◆ Provide a solution to the complaint only after careful consideration.
◆ Contact the customer after any agreed action has been completed to ensure that they are totally satisfied.
◆ Never be afraid to apologise.

There has been extensive research into complaint handling and the effect that it can have on consumer behaviour. This research did not concentrate on any particular market area but was based on a wide variety of consumers across the board. Consider the following statistics:

◆ Consumers are dissatisfied with purchases approximately 25% of the time.
◆ Of those consumers only 5% actually made a complaint. The remaining 95% either felt it was not worth complaining or did not know how and who to complain to.

◆ Only 50% of those who complain are satisfied with the way the complaint was handled.

◆ On average a satisfied consumer will tell another 3 people about their satisfaction.

◆ On average a dissatisfied consumer will tell 11 people about their complaint.

◆ Approximately 34% of consumers who complain will use the same business again provided their complaint is satisfactorily dealt with.

◆ If the complaint is resolved speedily and without undue fuss the previous figure of 34% can rise to up to 95% of people who will use the business again.

> **TIP**
>
> Sooner or later you will receive a complaint and it is extremely important that you have a strategy in place to deal with it.

INTRODUCING A QUALITY MANAGEMENT SYSTEM

Earlier in this chapter I outlined that it is not necessary to have a formal quality management system in place within your business. It will depend on the size of your business and the processes or procedures involved. As your business grows, however, you may wish to consider gaining formal quality accreditation. In some circumstances, formal accreditation will be required if you are to trade with large businesses.

By far the largest standard of qualification is that offered by the British Standards Institution under ISO9000:2000. Previously entitled BS5750, this is an independent endorsement that your business operates a quality management system that complies with the requirements of the standard.

In line with international efforts to harmonise systems and standards world-wide, ISO9000:2000 has the standing of both a British Standard (BS) and a Euro Norm (EN).

The standard was completely restructured and reissued in December 2000 to simplify the previous frameworks from 1987 and 1994 and it is now divided into three parts:

◆ ISO9000 – covers concepts, terminology and vocabulary.
◆ ISO9001 – specifies the requirements for a Quality Management System to meet this standard.
◆ ISO9004 – comprises a set of guidelines for continuous quality improvement. An associated standard, ISO19011, provides guidance on auditing both Quality Management Systems and Environmental Management Systems.

Key Sections of ISO9001:2000

ISO9001:2000 consists of eight sections, each of which has a number of sub-sections. The first three are for definition only, while the remaining five are central to developing a Quality Management System:

◆ Section Four – Quality Management System – the absolute foundation of the system. Concerned entirely with processes and documentation.
◆ Section Five – Management Responsibility – sets out the management responsibilities for running and controlling the system.
◆ Section Six – Resource Management – covers the provision of resources to implement and improve the system.
◆ Section Seven – Product Realisation – centres on processes and planning for converting inputs, for example raw materials and information, into products or service outputs.
◆ Section Eight – Measurement, Analysis and Improvement – focuses on how an organisation measures performance, and uses that analysis for continuous inprovement.

All of these sections are mandatory, except for Section Seven, which can be tailored to suit a particular business, Some sections will be easier to apply than others, and can be adapted to suit different sizes and types of businesses.

How long does accreditation take?

To a large extent this will depend on the size and complexity of your business. In general terms, most businesses seeking accreditation will take some nine to 18 months before they can achieve the standard.

How much does it cost?

This will also depend on your business and can vary quite substantially. It would be unrealistic for me even to give you a rough estimate. You also need to bear in mind that accreditation is not a one-off process. Once you have gained accreditation you will be visited each year by the certifying authority to ensure that you are still meeting the quality standard. Apart from the direct costs there are also indirect costs to consider, for example:

◆ staff time
◆ additional training.

TIP

Contact your local Business Link if you are considering accreditation – there may be a subsidy available to help pay for the services of a specialist consultant.

Where do I start?

Your first step is to identify a certification body whose scope of accreditation includes your type of business. All certification bodies are themselves accredited by the UK Accreditation Service and you should contact them to obtain guidance and assistance.

You must be under no illusions. Gaining ISO9000 is expensive, time consuming and extremely demanding. However, the benefits that your business will gain will outweigh all the pain involved. Even if you do not choose to implement a formal system, by having a positive attitude to quality and making sure that your customers are aware of it, your business will reap the rewards.

21 Exporting for the First Time

Most small businesses have no interest in exporting. With the world market becoming more and more accessible, however, you cannot afford to ignore it. I am not suggesting that you should look at exporting as soon as you start your business, rather that there may be opportunities for you to sell your products or services abroad.

In my own business, with the broadening of the consultancy market via the Internet I have a number of clients across the world. Some of these I have met personally and with others our only form of communication has been by telephone and e-mail. In actual fact, my 'export' sales now form a significant part of my business.

WHY SHOULD YOU CONSIDER EXPORTING?

There can be no doubt that in trading terms the world is getting smaller. Communication techniques have become more sophisticated, travel costs have fallen and substantially more trade information is available to break down the previous physical barriers involved with exporting. Whilst the vast majority of export sales from the UK are achieved by large companies there are still many opportunities for small businesses.

You need only consider the annual winners of the Queen's Award for Export. Surprisingly, most of the firms who win this award are small. Small businesses can also offer important competitive advantages in the export market. Larger firms tend to be more bureaucratic and less adaptable to changing market conditions. Small businesses, however,

TIP

Do not think that large overseas firms will only deal with other large businesses. Direct personal contact with the owner of a small business can be a major feature in persuading a large overseas business to become a customer.

tend to be more creative and more adaptable with the ability to respond quickly to the demands of their customers.

As you would expect there are numerous advantages and disadvantages to exporting. Each business will be different in terms of the ease with which exporting can be introduced and the difficulties that will be faced. Some of the benefits and disadvantages that were mentioned in research conducted amongst firms that export are given below.

Benefits of exporting

◆ Potential for increased profitability through additional sales
◆ Creation of new markets and new customers
◆ Less dependence on the 'home' market
◆ Enhancement of the business's reputation
◆ Increase in production leading to economies of scale
◆ Products that are saturated in the 'home' market are given a new outlet.

Disadvantages of exporting

◆ Financial risks due to currency fluctuations
◆ Drain on existing business resources
◆ Difficulties involved in dealing with 'unknown' third parties
◆ Potential of neglecting the 'home' market
◆ Language barriers
◆ Unrealistic expectations in terms of sales volumes
◆ Risks with regard to credit controls and bad debts
◆ Excessive costs in converting existing products to meet the demands of the export market.

IDENTIFYING EXPORT OPPORTUNITIES

Only you can decide whether exporting is right for your business. Once you have made the decision it is important that you take adequate time to identify the market, or markets, into which you propose to export.

Where can you export to?

To some extent this may depend on your products or services. Provided there is a demand, you can sell your products or services anywhere in the world. That assumes that there are no restrictions, for example, governmental or religious, that would prohibit you from exporting into a country.

There are a number of organisations that can help you with sourcing an export market including:

◆ The Department of Trade and Industry
◆ British Chambers of Commerce
◆ British Embassies
◆ The British Exporters Association
◆ Export Market Information Centre.

The Department of Trade and Industry (Dti)

Through Trade Partners UK the Dti offers a wide range of services for businesses seeking to export. These fall under six main headings:

◆ advice on the processes involved with exporting
◆ advice and assistance with market research
◆ assistance with export promotion
◆ help with identifying appropriate contacts abroad

- ◆ guidance on countering problems with the language barrier
- ◆ provision of potential leads for export opportunities.

TIP

The initial contact point for any business wishing to take advantage of the services offered by the Dti will be through the local Business Link.

British Chambers of Commerce

The Chambers of Commerce are extremely active in assisting their members with export opportunities. They organise a number of trade missions and fairs each year, many in conjunction with other trade associations. In some circumstances they also offer a subsidy to the costs involved with attending such functions.

British Embassies

Information and research on export opportunities can be gained from the embassies abroad through the Foreign and Commonwealth Office. They can also provide local expertise and assistance with any language barriers, as well as being a useful source of information on any import and export legislation that may affect you.

You can also commission tailored reports from the overseas embassies to answer specific queries. These could include reports on potential competitors, advice on promotion methods, and advice on suitable contacts. There is a fee for the provision of these reports.

The British Exporters Association (BEA)

Members of the association include export houses and distributors. The association seeks to link businesses wishing to export for the first time with their existing members who would be of most use.

The BEA produces a directory of export buyers in the UK which is divided into three main sections:

◆ a contact list of export buyers with the products, services and export markets that they cover

◆ a listing on a product basis

◆ a listing on a territorial market basis.

In addition, the association produces a regular 'Export Enquiry Circular' which enables businesses to make their products and export objectives known to other members.

Export Market Information Centre (EMIC)

EMIC provides library resources for businesses to undertake their own research into exporting. The information provided includes:

◆ **statistics** – trade, production, prices, employment, population and transport

◆ **country profiles** – general background together with economic, political and social information

◆ **foreign trade directories**, including local telephone directories

◆ **market research reports** covering major markets

◆ **development plans** – a guide to the current and future state of the economy

◆ **visitor plans and street guides**.

> **TIP**
>
> Even if you cannot personally attend the library you can still use one of their researchers to gather information for you, although there will be a fee involved. The results of the research will generally be available the same day.

STARTING TO EXPORT

Exporting is not an activity that should be undertaken lightly. You cannot afford to start without receiving substantial help and guidance. You must seek professional assistance.

Is your business ready to export?

Exporting can be very rewarding but it can also be costly. You will need to ensure that your business has the necessary information and available resources to succeed. These will fall under four key headings:

◆ knowledge of the market
◆ production capability to meet the new demand
◆ financial resources to cover initial increased costs
◆ management and staff resources.

Exporting will require thorough planning and you will need to write a detailed business plan with appropriate financial forecasts. It is absolutely essential that you go through the process of analysis, choice and implementation that was outlined in Chapter 4.

How will I enter the export market?

You have two basic choices, direct or indirect.

Direct

Direct exporting means that you will develop your own business into foreign markets. This method will require a lot of preparation with a significant investment in terms of both time and money. Essentially, you make the choice to manage the whole export process yourself although you may employ someone to assist you. Such a method might include the use of:

◆ agents
◆ distributors
◆ joint ventures
◆ trade fairs.

As an alternative, depending on your product, you may be able to sell direct to individuals or outlets abroad. This could be appropriate if the customer base is small or where the product is highly priced and there are few sales involved, as an example, luxury goods stocked by a limited number of outlets.

Indirect

This method involves selling your products to customers in the UK who then export them abroad. For obvious reasons this obviates the need for the complex processes involved with exporting. It does, however, introduce a 'middleman' and your profit margin will therefore be reduced. Examples include:

◆ **buying houses** – large foreign businesses with representation in the UK who purchase goods to be sold in their outlets abroad
◆ **export merchants** – businesses that buy direct from manufacturers and then sell the products to other businesses abroad.

> **TIP**
>
> Whichever method you choose, make sure you seek legal advice regarding any contract – agency legislation is extremely complex and you must remember that you could be liable for the actions of your agent.

MANAGING THE EXPORT PROCESS

If you decide that you are going to export your products yourself then you are going to have to deal with a number of physical aspects. Primarily these will involve the practical aspects of introducing your products into the export market. Specifically these will include:

◆ **Arranging transportation** – you will need to obtain the services of a freight forwarder to undertake the physical delivery of your products.
◆ **Ensuring suitable packaging** – you will need to review your packaging to ensure that your products will not be damaged in transit.

◆ **Raising the necessary documentation** – simple errors in documentation can lead to substantial delays at overseas customs; a good freight forwarder will help to ensure that your documentation is in order.

◆ **Establishing the terms of delivery** – it must be clear at what stage responsibility for your products passes from you to the overseas buyer.

Making sure you get paid

It is absolutely vital that you manage the way in which you receive payment. It is for you to specify the terms and conditions of trade and you should not feel pressurised into accepting terms that may be unfavourable. Remember – if you sell on credit then make sure that your customer will be able to make payment. There are a number of options that you have for receiving payment. A brief description of some of these is given below, but you should seek the advice of your own bank. They will have a specialist section that can give you specific advice based on the nature of your business.

> **TIP**
>
> Always treat large unsolicited export orders with extreme caution – many businesses lose money each year to fraudsters who take delivery of goods then disappear without making payment.

Cash in advance

For fairly obvious reasons this method of payment carries no risk to you. If you are dealing with an unknown customer, who perhaps has made an unsolicited approach to purchase your products, there is no reason why you should not ask for payment in advance.

Documentary letters of credit

These come in a number of different forms. In all cases they should be stated as being issued in accordance with the ICC Uniform Customs and Practice for Documentary Credits. This means the buyer arranges a credit with their bank and upon receipt of the correct documentation the bank makes payment direct to you. Payment can therefore be made as soon as the goods have been despatched.

The use of documentary credits for exports is extensive and it is a secure method of ensuring that you obtain payment. The documentation must be absolutely accurate because any errors can result in non-payment.

Bills of exchange

These may be used in conjunction with documentary credits where payment is not to be made immediately but at some future date. The documents of title to the goods are despatched by your bank, together with the bill of exchange, direct to the purchaser's bank. There are two different arrangements that can be made:

◆ **Documents against payment (DP)** – the documents of title to the goods are only passed to the purchaser once payment for the goods has been made.
◆ **Documents against acceptance (DA)** – the documents are passed to the purchaser once the bill of exchange has been 'accepted' for payment. Once 'accepted', payment cannot be countermanded.

Open account

Once a customer becomes established you may wish to offer the same terms that you offer to your 'home market' customers. Effectively, the goods are despatched and then an invoice is sent for payment. This arrangement does carry the most degree of risk but in appropriate circumstances it is a cheap and easy-to-administer option. It removes the costs of arranging documentary credits and/or bills of exchange.

Dealing with exchange rate risks

When you price your goods in a foreign market you will have to decide whether you will accept payment in pounds sterling or the currency of the country involved. In some cases, certainly if exporting to developing countries, you may wish to price your products in an alternative currency, for example, US dollars.

> **TIP**
>
> If the rate fluctuates widely then you could find that your entire profit margin has been wiped out and your exports have actually cost you money.

You must recognise that if you price your products in a specific currency then you are taking a risk. If the exchange rate fluctuates then you could lose, or even make money.

It is important that you seek the advice of your bank if your exports are significant. There are a number of options that they may recommend:

◆ **Forward exchange options** – an option entered into with your bank to buy or sell, a specific amount of foreign currency on a specific date. This then sets the exchange rate for the business transaction and gives you a firm foundation on which to price your goods.

◆ **Currency account** – the establishment of an account in a foreign currency into which you can pay the proceeds of your exports. If appropriate, you can also draw on this account to pay any expenses incurred in the country into which you are exporting. These could include agents' commissions, distribution or promotion costs.

ARRANGING INSURANCE

Credit insurance is a vital part of the planning process and it should be included in all of your costings when looking at a potential market. Quite apart from the risks of non-payment, insurance should be obtained to cover risks that would not be included in your standard commercial policy. For example, you may find that your products are not insured against loss at sea.

In addition to offering appropriate export insurance, many specialist brokers also offer a number of support services. This could include credit and trade reference information on your potential new customers. This information could prove invaluable and save you time and money in the long run.

There is also a government agency, The Export Credit Guarantee Department (ECGD) that may be able to offer assistance. They provide insurance for capital goods where long-term credit arrangements of two years and over are involved.

> **TIP**
>
> As with all forms of insurance make sure that the policy actually covers the risks that you want to insure – read the small print carefully for exclusions.

22

Dealing With Problems

At some stage of running your business you are going to encounter problems. The level of impact that they have on your business will depend to a certain degree on what contingency plans you have in place to deal with them. Problems will not be just financial. They could be non-financial but have just as devastating an effect as financial problems. In this chapter we will look at some of the problems that could occur and what sort of strategies you can have in place to deal with them.

FORMULATING CONTINGENCY PLANS

Problems can be minimised before a crisis occurs through forward planning. You will need to devise and implement everyday business procedures to minimise the chances of a crisis occurring in the first place. You will also want to work out what you should do if any particular crisis does occur.

The important part of planning is to take time to identify the possible crises that may affect your business. Think through why they might occur and how you can prevent this. Consider how they would affect you and what has to be done to put things right if they happen despite your precautions.

> **TIP**
>
> It is much easier to think through all of the possibilities if you can involve other people.

Being prepared for a crisis

Crises can be classified into two main groups: external and internal.

External crises are those which are outside the control of the business but which affect the business environment. External crises may include family problems or a bankrupt client leaving bad debts and order cancellations. More extreme examples of external crises are often classed as disasters, e.g. fire, flood, bomb alert, or explosion.

Internal crises are those which occur within the business. They often have little or no effect on the external environment. Examples include power or machinery failure, a computer crash, data corruption or something as simple as losing your diary.

> **TIP**
>
> It is absolutely essential that you have some form of crisis management plan which can be put into action as soon as a crisis occurs.

In the next section we will look at the specific problems of dealing with problem debtors, the most common financial crisis likely to affect you. For the moment we need to concentrate on some of the ways that you can mitigate the non-financial problems that could occur.

A crisis of any degree can have an adverse affect on a business, ranging from disruptive to devastating. If not properly managed, a crisis can lead to loss of earnings, reduction in profits and ultimately, may cause the business to go bankrupt. The damage caused by a crisis can, however, be minimised.

All possible remedial actions – for example, the procedures and personal areas of responsibility of key employees – should be considered to work out the best course of action in any given crisis. There are four key areas that you will need to consider:

◆ **identification** of the potential crisis
◆ gathering all possible **information** about the crisis and the circumstances which may lead up to it

TIP

The contingency plan should be regularly revised, particularly after a crisis, so that it can be improved through the lessons that have been learned.

◆ **isolating** the crisis

◆ what **action** can be taken to resolve the crisis and any damage caused by it.

A draft contingency plan can then be drawn up and tested. Once this has been carried out the plans should be documented in a form that is easily accessible by all relevant staff.

Dealing with problem debtors

It is absolutely essential that you have a system in place to deal with all aspects of your debtor book. Before even granting any form of credit to a debtor, you will need to undertake some investigation as to their creditworthiness.

You should never be afraid of refusing credit if you are in any doubt. You may lose the sale but it is better to lose the profit element on this sale than the whole amount of the sale itself by way of a bad debt. Always remember, you have not completed the sale until you are actually paid. All you have done is taken a gamble – consider the odds carefully before you place your bet.

It is crucial that you have some formal procedures in place to monitor your debtors. Some of these include:

◆ The imposition of a credit limit for each customer which you should never allow them to exceed.

◆ The monitoring of regular payments to clear the debt – as soon as payment becomes due make sure that you chase it up.

◆ Once a payment becomes overdue do not allow further credit on the account – even if the credit limit has yet to be reached.

◆ If the debt becomes excessively overdue, for example, your credit terms are 30 days and the debt has now been outstanding 60 days, then write to the customer demanding immediate payment.

◆ Follow up your letter after seven days with a further demand and giving notice that if necessary you will take legal action.

◆ If payment has still not been received after a further seven days then you should immediately consider issuing a summons. For debts of up to £5,000 these can be easily issued through a County Court.

Never allow any one customer an excessive amount of credit. A number of small businesses fail each year because of bad debts incurred through dealing with apparently large stable companies that go to the wall.

> **TIP**
>
> Do not be fobbed off with excuses for non-payment. You must remember that even small bad debts can have a devastating impact on your profit margins.

Insuring against problems

You will need to seek specialist advice on exactly what type of insurance is relevant to your specific business. Examples of the type of insurance that may be applicable include:

◆ employer's liability insurance
◆ fire and other perils insurance
◆ theft insurance
◆ consequential loss insurance
◆ professional indemnity insurance
◆ keyperson insurance.

Employer's liability insurance

As an employer you must, by law, have employer's liability insurance. A copy of the relevant certificate of insurance must also be prominently displayed at all places of work.

Fire and other perils insurance

Adequate insurance to cover the possible destruction of your buildings and contents through fire is essential. You should also ensure that cover is in place for other perils, for example storm damage, flooding or explosions.

Theft insurance

This type of insurance will only normally cover thefts where a forced entry has been made. It does not usually cover such events as thefts by employees. If you do wish to insure against this you will need to arrange additional cover.

Consequential loss insurance

If your business does suffer a major catastrophe which effectively stops you trading for a time this type of cover will insure against the loss of profits. It may also cover your employee costs and the costs of establishing interim trading premises.

Professional indemnity insurance

If you are in a service-based business offering expert advice, it is essential that you have adequate professional indemnity insurance to cover you against claims by your clients for damages caused by your negligence. In some cases, it will be required in any event as a condition of your membership of a professional body.

Keyperson insurance

If you have one or more key members of staff on whom the business depends for success you should consider keyperson insurance. This will pay out a lump sum in the event of that person's death.

Personal insurance

It is advisable to consider personal insurance to cover yourself in the event of accident, sickness or death. If you are trading on your own you must remember that you may be unable to earn an income should anything happen that could affect your health.

Accident and sickness

You need to arrange an alternative income in the event of an unfortunate accident or short-term sickness. These policies will pay out a monthly amount and, for obvious reasons, you need to arrange sufficient insurance to ensure that the income will cover your expenditure. These policies should be reviewed annually and the insurance cover increased accordingly.

Critical illness

These policies will pay out a lump sum in the event of your being diagnosed with a life-threatening illness. They are similar to life policies but the lump sum is paid out as soon as a diagnosis is made. Payment is not dependant upon your death and, should the illness prove non-fatal, the lump sum is not repayable.

Death

It is relatively inexpensive to arrange a term life assurance policy for an adequate sum to pay off all of your debts. This is something that you need to consider extremely carefully, especially if you have a family, as in the absence of sufficient insurance cover, your debts will have to be met from your estate. This may involve the sale of assets that you own which are also an important part of your family's life.

TIP

Loan protection insurance offered by some banks can be expensive for what it offers – always obtain alternative quotations.

AVOIDING DISASTER

It is an established statistic that businesses are more likely to fail in their first five years of trading. The chances of success increase the older and more experienced the business, and the management, but, it can take up to ten years before the business is on a firm foundation.

One of the major causes of failure is inexperience in managing all aspects of running a business at the same time. You may be a first class plumber but unless you manage your time and your work quotations in order to make a profit you will fail in business. Unfortunately many business owners are quick to blame others when the actual cause of failure is their own shortcomings. The bank manager features highly on the list of causes being blamed for the business failure due to the lack of provision of additional finance.

Reasons for failure

In surveys conducted amongst small businesses, the common reasons for failure were cited as:

◆ further funding being turned down
◆ lack of sales
◆ late payment by debtors – cash flow problems
◆ increased competition from larger firms.

Professional advisors, however, have a totally different view on the major causes of failure – they place the blame squarely on poor management. The reasons that they give include:

◆ Lack of capital.
◆ Targets are not set and properly reviewed.
◆ Performance, especially financial, is not monitored.

- Corrective action, if any, is taken far too late.
- Market research is not kept up to date.
- Turnover is chased instead of profit.

The last of these, often referred to as 'overtrading', is not recognised at all by some businesses. They consider that they must increase turnover as quickly as possible although they lack the working capital to support the expansion.

Have a clear way forward

There are a number of things that you can do to help you succeed. Businesses that seek professional advice and training on running their business tend to have a greater survival rate. You can see from the list of reasons above given by professional advisors the sort of planning that you should be doing. In simple terms, once you have established your business you need to:

- Update your original business plan on a regular basis.
- Constantly monitor your financial performance to enable early corrective action to be taken.
- Concentrate on making a profit and not just the volume of sales.
- Take advantage of as much training in all aspects of running a business as you can – in most cases it is offered free of charge or at a very small cost.
- Keep looking at conditions in the market – do not be caught out by the actions of competitors which could remove your competitive advantage.

23

Staying Ahead of the Competition

Maintaining your unique selling point and competitive advantage through ongoing market intelligence and competitor information is vital. Up-to-date information about your market will keep you aware of changes or developments that could affect your business, at the same time indicating trends in consumer demand that you can exploit. It could also help you to identify economic trends in the market that could affect the buying habits of your customers.

Using market intelligence

Market intelligence will enable you to update your sales forecasts on a regular basis, also assisting you when reviewing your overall strategy. It is also critical that you keep track of your competitors. On a continuing basis you need to find out what they are doing, what they are charging, and any new products they have launched which could compete with yours. Even if you consider that your product is the best in the market there will always be someone competing with you on a different factor of the marketing mix.

If you employ sales staff, ensure that they obtain feedback from your customers. It is likely that your customers will also be looking at the activities of your competitors and it may be that they can provide you with 'inside' information. For example, it is not unknown for a competitor to approach a customer of a rival firm and offer some form of inducement such as a discount or better credit terms in order to gain their business. Lack of information on this sort of activity at an early stage could lead to your customer base declining.

Retaining competitive advantage

Competitive advantage is everything in business. You must retain a unique selling point that will consistently bring you new customers as well as repeat business. The only way you can do this is to research the market continually in order to establish exactly what is happening.

Information is power and unless you have that power you may miss out on new opportunities available to you in the market. Even worse, you could succumb to new threats in the market that could destroy your business.

> **TIP**
>
> You must take all necessary action to ensure that you stay ahead of the competition.

Avoid complacency at all costs

There will never be a time when you can afford to do nothing within your business. There will always be something that you can do better or more efficiently. It does not matter what size of business you run. If you do not do it, someone else will step in and fill the gap. You only need to compare the stock exchange listings from ten years ago with those of today to find a lot of missing names – some of them even household names at the time.

Failure in business can happen to anyone and whilst many would blame lack of resources, there can only be one true reason. They were not providing what the customer wanted, at the right price and at the right time. In essence, their marketing failed.

ESTABLISHING A MANAGEMENT INFORMATION SYSTEM

Management information comes in a variety of formats. You need to establish a management information system as an entirely distinct function within your business, and allocate sufficient time and resources to ensure that it is effective.

The cost of computers continuing to fall as they have done in recent years, there is no excuse for not having a computer and a printer for your business. The availability of suitable database software makes this the most efficient way of storing information, as well as giving you the added advantage of being able to organise the information in many different ways. These aspects are considered in Chapter 24.

> **TIP**
>
> There is little point in keeping track of information within the system when you have no idea of what use you will put that information to in the future.

You do, however, need to be aware of the 'paralysis by analysis' maxim. This refers to spending so much time evaluating past performance that you lose track of your overall plan. Prioritising information is essential in keeping the whole management information system workable.

Decide which information is critical to oversee the overall business operation and then store only that which is appropriate to meet that objective. The simpler the system, the more likely it will be to succeed.

You need to ask yourself three questions when establishing your management information system:

◆ What information do I need?
◆ Why do I need it?
◆ What will I use it for?

Unless you can provide satisfactory answers for all three questions for any piece of information there is probably little value in storing it. At all costs, avoid storing information which you 'think I might need in the future'. If you do need something similar in the future you should be able to obtain more up-to-date information.

The introduction of a management information system, especially where it affects or measures human performance, can be a very sensitive issue. A possible example could be where you are measuring the sales performance of your staff. Take time to explain the purpose of the system to your staff and seek their help in design and implementation.

TIP

Keeping your staff in the dark will more than likely cause a reduction in morale leading to possible operational problems. This could, in turn, lead to a downturn in productivity and sales.

Use your staff to gather information for you. Many items of critical marketing intelligence are lost because staff do not see the need to report it. For example, if you have delivery staff use them to gain intelligence when they deliver goods. They can probably see the efforts of your competitors who are also delivering goods and this information could provide opportunities for you.

You may have no need actually to store the information in the management information system. It is, however, better to have it in the first place and subsequently discard it, than not to have it at all. Competitive advantage is critical, and to maintain that advantage you must obtain ongoing information on what is happening in the market.

UPDATING YOUR BUSINESS PLAN

As soon as you have completed your original business plan it is immediately out of date. In the time taken to research the market and put the plan together it is inevitable that conditions will have changed. This is something that you must recognise and do something about. Quite apart from regularly updating your market research and financial forecasts, you also need to look at all the other aspects of your business.

TIP

The most common aspect of business planning that is ignored when updating a business plan is the legislation that could affect a business – make sure you keep up to date.

Coping with change

To survive in business you regularly need to review the way in which
you do things. Constant innovations in technology and business
methods mean you need to stay abreast of what is happening. In the
final chapter we will deal with technology, but for the moment you
need to review all the other aspects of the PESTE analysis that were
considered in Chapter 4.

As part of retaining your competitive advantage you should always be
looking for ways in which you can improve your business. This
means that you must not be averse to changes. You cannot rely on
your customers retaining the tastes and preferences that they have
today. Some very large businesses have ignored this and suffered the
dire consequences.

A consultant can help your business in this area by giving an unbiased
opinion on the way in which you are conducting your business and
possible improvements that could be made. They will help to break
down the barriers that most businesses have to change and, probably
more essentially to you, suggest ways in which overall profitability
can be increased.

Learning to delegate responsibility

Over time your business will hopefully grow and it is important that
you have appropriate strategies to manage this
successfully. You must therefore learn to
delegate. As the business grows you will no
longer be able to do everything yourself. You
need to manage your time properly if you are
to avoid failure. Let us assume that your
business is in the service industry.

> **TIP**
>
> Do not become entrenched in
> your business methods – change
> is inevitable in all markets and
> you must stay one step ahead if
> you are to succeed.

As the business grows you will probably be able to offer less and less time to provide the service effectively. The day-to-day administration aspects will increase to such a point that they are eroding the time available for you to do what you are good at, i.e. providing the service. It is important that you recognise the possibility before it happens. Any deterioration in the standard of service that you provide could lead to you losing customers.

There can also be cost benefits in delegating properly. The costs of employing someone to look after basic administration can be covered by the extra time available to you to concentrate on trading. If you provide some form of service and charge £50 per hour based on an eight hour day it is costing you £400 in lost income for every day that you spend on 'unproductive' work. It is unlikely that you would pay a part-time employee that sort of amount to look after the basic administration for you.

TIP

Always consider the opportunity costs, i.e. the amount that you are losing against paying someone to do the work for you – it could have a major impact upon profitability if you can avoid wasting your time.

24

Using Technology in Your Business

Throughout this book I have emphasised the advantages of having a computer system to look after your management information. It does not matter what size or type of business you operate – a computer is an essential piece of equipment for you. Technology does not, of course, merely relate to computers. Other items of technology that you might use in your business include:

◆ telephones
◆ fax machines
◆ photocopiers
◆ mobile telephones.

When you start your business you should be thinking small. You will need to appraise critically whether a particular item of technology is absolutely essential. As a specific example I would caution you against either purchasing or leasing a photocopier, at least initially.

For some reason photocopiers can be very temperamental and there are other options available, such as a copy facility on a fax machine or computer printer. There are also numerous small shops where a photocopy service is offered at a minimal cost per page.

CHOOSING A COMPUTER SYSTEM

With the speed of change in the specifications of computer systems, it is impossible to recommend any basic system. There are, however, a number of things that you should consider because your computer may

provide the whole foundation of your business information and
management system:

◆ The **processor speed** may have little importance to you because it
will not be required to run complex games software. Although
processor speeds are increasing, indeed probably doubling every
year, you will not really require the latest model
◆ The **hard drive capacity** will be more important to you and it
should be as large as you can afford. You will not wish to run out of
space and then have to transfer all your files
to another system
◆ In terms of **RAM**, the more that you have the
better because it will speed up the running of
your applications. At the very least you should
look at a system with a minimum of 256MB.

> **TIP**
>
> When you choose a monitor
> make sure that you purchase one
> that is as large as you can afford.
> You will probably spend many
> hours in front of it.

Keeping duplicate records

This is often ignored by most businesses with computerised accounts.
There can be serious consequences if this task is not undertaken. You
cannot ignore the fact that technology does sometimes go wrong and
computers are no exception.

If I were to lose the information stored on my computer I would be
absolutely devastated. For this reason I have at least three back-up
copies stored in different places, including one on a totally remote
computer system. This means it is merely a minor irritation for me to
retrieve a back-up copy.

Making regular copies

You must make regular copies of your accounting records. At the very
least, this should be done once a week, although daily would be even

better. There are a number of different ways in which you can make copies. You can store a copy in a different place on your hard drive, although this in itself is not recommended. If a hard drive fails it usually affects the whole drive and not just segments of it.

A better method would to be use an alternative storage device, or example:

<table>
<tr><td>

TIP

Do not rely on floppy disks for long-term storage because they can be prone to failure. It is far better to spend time and money on an alternative system from the outset – you can then be sure that your records are safe.

</td><td>

◆ tape drive streamer
◆ zip disk
◆ CD-ROM.

All these alternatives are relatively cheap to purchase and are sometimes offered as part of the computer system. All offer a large volume of storage space, for example a CD-ROM will store at least 650Mb of information on each disk.

</td></tr>
</table>

Deciding on a printer

The appearance of your documents is important and, in my opinion, only a laser printer will produce the required quality. You probably do not require one that prints more than eight pages per minute nor one that can deal with anything other than black and white printing on standard A4 paper.

There are also a number of printers on the market which have additional functions, such as a combined scanner, copier and printer. These could be a cheaper alternative than purchasing the three items separately.

The cost of colour inkjet printers have also substantially reduced in recent years and a 'photo quality' printer could be useful if you are going to print your own publicity material. It is entirely a matter of personal choice. You will, of course, also need to consider the relative costs of replacement printer cartridges.

Considering the software that you will need

At the very minimum you will require word processing and spreadsheet programs and you may also wish to consider a database program. Choosing your software is very important. You need to choose software that will cope with your business demands for some time to come. There is very little point in purchasing software that will not, for example, allow a professional layout and style to your documents.

> **TIP**
>
> Always have a spare cartridge for your printer in stock. They always seem to run out at the most inopportune moment when a replacement may not be readily available.

If any software is being bundled with the purchase of a computer system it is unlikely to be very useful. Most packages concentrate on games programs with only the very basic 'business' software. Saving money on your software is not a good idea.

I would strongly recommend that you opt for one of the 'professional' packages offered by the larger computer software firms. This will give you a better platform on which to work and probably offer better presentation options. In addition, within the software there will normally be a number of predefined templates that you can use. These will give you a number of benefits:

> **TIP**
>
> Seek advice from your local Business Link when choosing a computer system and the software – you may find that a grant will be available or, at the very least, training in using the software.

◆ The ability to **design and print** letterheads and other documents such as invoices in a standardised format.

◆ The creation of **spreadsheets** to manage your financial forecasting and management accounts.

◆ A **database** to maintain details of all your clients and suppliers as part of your management information system.

TIP

There is no quality control on the information available on the Internet which means that anyone can publish anything. If you are going to rely on any piece of information you need to ensure that you obtain it from a reliable source.

USING THE INTERNET

The Internet provides a wealth of information produced by governments, businesses, academic institutions and individuals which can be extremely useful. It is an easy and fast method of obtaining both facts and opinions. Look at the contacts section at the end of this book to discover the help and assistance that is freely available to you.

Finding information on the Internet

Every website has its own address, known as a Uniform Resource Locator (URL). If you know the URL you can connect to the site by typing this address into your web browser. If you do not know the URL the easiest way to find a site is by using a search engine. Search engines check the contents of individual sites and index them accordingly. However, one search engine can never cover the entire content of the Internet.

To find a site, or information on a particular subject, you type in the name of the organisation or subject and the search engine will then display those sites that should cover the information you are trying to find. For obvious reasons this can be a little 'hit and miss'. If you make your request more specific you will increase the likelihood of finding relevant information. There are a number of search engines available including:

◆ Yahoo – www.yahoo.co.uk

◆ Altavista – www.altavista.com

◆ All the web – www.alltheweb.com

◆ Google – www.google.com

There are also other methods by which you can gain information:

Usenet

Usenet is a global conferencing system which enables people to communicate over the Internet. These conferences, normally referred to as newsgroups, deal with a wide variety of subjects. Usenet newsgroups that start with 'biz' deal with issues of relevance to businesses.

> **TIP**
>
> As a personal preference I use Google, which always seems to provide relevant sites very quickly. If you cannot find the information using one search engine then you can always try using another.

Each newsgroup contains articles that are similar to e-mail postings, each separate article kept in a subject folder with any replies. To access a newsgroup a reader is required which will usually be within your e-mail or browser software. You can also gain details of all the newsgroups available to you from your Internet Service Provider (ISP).

Always read the 'frequently asked questions' (FAQs) first to check whether the subject you are searching for has already been covered. Most newsgroups also have rules or 'netiquette' which need to be followed. Newsgroups, unfortunately, are used by 'spammers' to gain e-mail addresses. If you do post anything then sooner or later you can expect to receive unwanted junk e-mails.

> **TIP**
>
> When posting to a newsgroup never use your permanent e-mail address – use a free address e.g. those available from Yahoo.com or Bigfoot.com which can be 'thrown away' if necessary.

Mailing lists

Mailing lists are useful for discussions on current issues and for obtaining advice or information from other people who are subscribed to the list. Lists are controlled by mail servers that copy a message from one person to all the others that are subscribed.

> **TIP**
>
> Remember that anyone can subscribe to a mailing list and contribute. Do not always rely on the advice you might receive in response to a question.

There are thousands of mailing lists on the Internet that are available for public subscription. I would strongly suggest you subscribe to one list at a time because some lists are more active than others. I personally subscribe to a list that generates anything from 50 to 150 e-mails per day. You can find details of mailing lists that are relevant to businesses, and indeed any other subjects that may interest you at www.liszt.com.

Sourcing business on the Internet

The Internet could also be a useful source of business for you. The present government is committed to encouraging more small businesses to tender for work and a wealth of information in this respect is available. In a similar way, Local Authorities are being encouraged to advertise tender opportunities for all manner of goods and services.

With the breakdown in trade barriers there are also tender opportunities for many businesses across the world. Organisations such as the World Bank and the International Monetary Fund regularly place opprtunities on their respective websites, British Embassies abroad are also a source of sales leads which are passed back to Trade Partners UK. If you register with them, free of charge, they will provide leads via e-mail for whatever type of products you wish to supply.

With more and more business being conducted via the Internet it is essential that you maximise the opportunities that are available.

Useful Contacts

Advertising Association, Abford House, 15 Wilton Road, London SW1V 1NJ.
Tel: (020) 7828 2771. Fax: (020) 7931 0376. Website: www.adassoc.org

Advertising Standards Authority, 2 Torrington Place, London WC1E 7HW.
Tel: (020) 7580 5555. Fax: (020) 7631 3051. Website: www.asa.org.uk

Advisory Conciliation and Advisory Service (ACAS)
National Helpline: 08457 47 47 47. Website: www.acas.org.uk

Association of British Insurers, 51 Gresham Street, London EC2V 7HQ.
Tel: (020) 7700 3333. Fax: (020) 7696 8999. Website: www.abi.org.uk

Association of Business Recovery Professionals. Website: www.r3.org.uk

Association of Chartered Certified Accountants, 29 Lincoln's Inn Fields, London, WC2A 3EE.
Tel: (020) 7242 6855. Website: www.acca.org.uk

Better Payment Practice Group. Website: www.payontime.co.uk

British Bankers Association. Website: www.bba.org.uk

British Chambers of Commerce, Manning House, 22 Carlisle Place, London SW1P 1JA.
Tel: (020) 7565 2000. Website: www.britishchambers.org.uk

British Exporters Association, Broadway House, Tothill Street, London SW1H 9NQ.
Tel: (020) 7799 2468.

The British Franchise Association, Thames View, Newtown Road, Henley on Thames
Oxon RG9 1 HG.
Tel: (01491) 578050. Fax: (01491) 573517. Website: www.british-franchise.org.uk

Business Franchise Directory, Miller Freeman, Blenheim House, 630 Chiswick High Road,
London W4 5BG. Tel: (020) 8742 2828.

Business Hotline Publications. Website: www.bizhot.co.uk

British Library Business Information Research Service, 25 Southampton Buildings, London WC2A 1AW. Tel: (020) 7412 7457. Fax: (020) 7412 7453.

Business Names Registrations plc, Somerset House, Temple Street, Birmingham B2 5DN. Tel: (0121) 643 0227.

British Venture Capital Association, Essex House, 12–13 Essex Street, London WC2R 3AA. Tel: (020) 7240 3846. Website: www.bvca.co.uk

Business Link Network. Tel: 0845 600 9006. Website: www.businesslink.gov.uk

Business Zone. Website: www.businesszone.co.uk

Chartered Institute of Management Accountants, 63 Portland Place, London, W1N 4AB Tel: (020) 7917 9256. Website: www.cimaglobal.com

The Chartered Institute of Marketing, Moor Hall, Cookham, Maidenhead, Berkshire SL6 9QH. Tel (01628) 427 500. Fax (01628) 427 349. Website www.cim.co.uk

The Chartered Institute of Patent Agents, Staple Inn Buildings, High Holborn, London WC1V 7PZ. Tel: (020) 7405 9450. Website: www.cipa.org.uk

City and Guilds of London Institute. Website: www.city-and-guilds.co.uk

Companies House, Crown Way, Cardiff CF14 3UZ. Tel: (02920) 388588. Website: www.companies-house.gov.uk

Confederation of British Industry (CBI). Website: www.cbi.org.uk

Credit Protection Association. Website: www.cpa.co.uk

Data Protection Registrar. Website: www.informationcommissioner.gov.uk

Department of Trade and Industry. Website: www.dti.gov.uk

Department of Trade and Industry, Publications Orderline, Admail 528, London SW1W 8YT. Tel: 0870 150 2500. Website: www.dti.gov.uk/publications

Direct Marketing Association, (Fax Preference Service – FPS), (Tel Preference Service – TPS), Haymarket House, 1 Oxendon Street, London SW1Y 4EE. Tel: (020) 7321 2525. Fax: (020) 7321 0191. Website: www.dma.org.uk

European Structural Funds. Website: www.dti.gov.uk/europe/structural.html

Export Market Information Centre, Kingsgate House, 66–74 Victoria Street, London SW1E 6SW. Tel: (020) 7215 5444. Fax: (020) 7215 4231. Website: www.tradepartners.gov.uk

European Union Information. Website: www.europa.eu.int

European Union Tender Information Search. Website: www.ted.publications.eu.int

Federation of Small Businesses, Whittle Way, Blackpool Business Park, Blackpool, Lancashire FY4 2FE.
Tel: (01253) 336000. Website: www.fsb.org.uk

Forum of Private Business, Ruskin Chambers, Drury Lane, Knutsford, Cheshire WA16 7BR.
Tel: (01565) 634467. Website: www.fpb.co.uk

The Franchise Business, 6 Wight View, Bembridge Drive, Hayling Island, Hampshire. PO11 9LU.
Tel: (023) 9246 2111. Fax: (023) 9246 3555. Website: www.franchisebusiness.co.uk

Franchise World Magazine, James House, 37 Nottingham Road, London, SW17 7EA.
Tel: (020) 8767 1371. Website: www.franchiseworld.co.uk

Government Information Service. Website: www.open.gov.uk

Grants and Funding Information. Websites: www.grantsnet.co.uk, www.j4b.co.uk

Grant for Research and Development. Website: www.dti.gov.uk/r-d/

Health and Safety Executive Information Centre.
Tel: (0870) 154 5500. Website: www.hse.gov.uk

Health and Safety Executive Publications, P O Box 1999, Sudbury, Suffolk CO10 2WA.
Tel: (01787) 881165. Website: www.hsebooks.co.uk

HM Customs and Excise – National Advice Service.
Tel: (0845) 010 9000. Website: www.hmce.gov.uk

Inland Revenue New Employers Helpline.
Tel: (0845) 60 70 143. Website: www.inlandrevenue.gov.uk

Innovation Unit. Website: www.innovation.gov.uk

Institute of Chartered Accountants in England and Wales, P O Box 433, Chartered Accountants Halls, Moorgate Place, London, EC2P 2BJ.
Tel: (020) 7920 8100. Website: www.icaew.co.uk

Institute of Chartered Accountants of Scotland, 27 Queen Street, Edinburgh, EH2 1LA.
Tel: (0131) 225 5673. Website: www.icas.org.uk

Institute of British Exporters. Website: www.export.co.uk

Institute of Quality Assurance. Website: www.iqa.org

The Institute of Trade Mark Agents, Canterbury House, 2–6 Sydenham Road, Croydon, Surrey CR0 9XE. Tel: (020) 8686 2052.

Jordans Market Surveys, 21 St. Thomas Street, Bristol, Avon BS1 6JS.
Tel: (0117) 923 0600. Fax: (0117) 923 0063.

Key Note Reports, ICC Publications Ltd, Field House, 72 Oldfield Road, Hampton, Middlesex, TW12 2HQ.
Tel: (020) 8481 8750. Fax: (020) 8783 0049. Website: www.keynote.co.uk

Lawyers For Your Business, The Law Society, Freepost WC2576, London WC2A 1BR. Tel: (020) 7405 9075. Website: www.lfyb.lawsociety.org.uk

Mailing Preference Service, 5 Reef House, Plantation Wharf, London SW13 3UF.
Tel: (020) 7738 1625.

Market Assessment Publications Ltd, 5th Floor, 110 Strand, London WC2R 0AA.
Tel: (020) 7836 5111. Fax: (020) 7836 5222.

Market Research Society, 15 Northburgh Street, London EC1V 0AH.
Tel: (020) 7490 4911. Fax: (020) 7490 0608. E-mail: info@marketresearch.org.uk
Website: www.marketresearch.org.uk

Mintel International Group Ltd, 18–19 Long Lane, London EC1A 9HE.
Tel: (020) 7606 6000. Fax: (020) 7606 5932. E-mail: enquiries@mintel.co.uk
Website: www.mintel.co.uk

National Business Angels Network, 40–42 Cannon Street, London, EC4N 6JJ.
Tel: (020) 7329 4141. Website: www.nationalbusangels.co.uk

National Federation of Enterprise Agencies, Trinity Gardens, 9–11 Bromham Road, Bedford, MK40 2UQ. Tel: (01234) 354 055. Website: www.nfea.com

The National Franchise Exhibition. Website: www.nfe.co.uk

Office of Fair Trading. Website: www.oft.gov.uk

Office for National Statistics, Government Buildings, Cardiff Road, Newport, Gwent NP9 1XG.
Tel: (01633) 812 973. Fax: (01633) 812 599. E-mail: library@ons.gov.uk
(Economic and business statistics)

Office for National Statistics, 1 Drummond Gate, London SW1V 2QQ.
Tel: (020) 7533 6260. Fax: (020) 7533 6261. E-mail: info@ons.gov.uk
(Population, health and social statistics). Website: www.statistics.co.uk

The Patent Office. Tel: (0645) 500505. E-mail: enquiries@patent.gov.uk
Website: www.patent.gov.uk

The Prince's Trust Website: www.princes-trust.org.uk

Reed Business Information. Website: www.reedinfo.co.uk

Royal Mail. Website. www.royalmail.co.uk

Shell *Live*WIRE, Hawthorn House, Forth Banks, Newcastle-upon-Tyne NE1 3SG.
Tel: (08457) 573252. Website: www.shell-livewire.org

Small Business Service. Website: www.businessadviceonline.org
Small Firms Loan Guarantee Scheme. Tel. 0845 001 0032. Website: www.dti.gov.uk/sflg/
Society of Procurement Officers. Website: www.sopo.org
Trade Partners UK. Website: www.tradepartners.gov.uk

UK Accreditation Service, 21–47 High Street, Feltham, Middlesex TW13 4UN.
Tel: (020) 8917 8400. Website: www.ukas.com

UK Business Incubation. Website: www.ukbi.co.uk

UK Trade Fairs and Exhibitions. Website: www.exhibitions.co.uk

Alan Le Marinel, Parkstone Management Consultancy. Website: www.pkstone.co.uk

Glossary

ACAS *See* Advisory, Conciliation and Arbitration Service.

ACCA The Association of Chartered Certified Accountants.

Accounts Financial records of a business.

Accruals Revenue and costs which are recognised in the accounts for the period in which they are earned or incurred – which may not be the same period in which payment is received or made.

Acid Test Ratio *See* Quick Ratio.

Administrative receiver A person who, under certain circumstances, takes control of all the company's assets in order to try to pay off the company's debt without it going into liquidation.

Advisory, Conciliation and Arbitration Service A body providing intermediary services to help resolve disputes between employers and their employees.

Agent A person who is acting on someone else's behalf, e.g. in business transactions.

Amortisation Writing off an asset over a period. Can also be referred to as depreciation.

Annual return Every company having a share capital must supply basic information to the Registrar of Companies once a year and this is known as the 'annual return'.

Appraisal Process of assessing how well someone or something is suited to a purpose.

Appropriation Account The part of the profit and loss account which explains how the profit has been divided or appropriated.

Arbitration Process Where a dispute is taken to an independent third party (e.g. ACAS) for judgement; both parties in dispute will have agreed to abide by any decision made.

Articles of Association A document detailing internal regulations for a company, signed by the subscribers. It indicates the powers of directors and shareholders – individually and in meetings and rules for the transfer and allotment of shares.

ASA The Advertising Standards Authority.

Association cause This is a clause within the Memorandum of Association of a company where the subscribers state that they have joined together to form the company.

Audit A thorough annual review of company accounts to determine their accuracy. Audits must be undertaken by an accountant who is an authorised auditor.

Authorised capital Maximum share capital a company is allowed to issue under its articles of association.

Backups Computer file copies made to be kept in case the originals are lost.

Bad debts Debts which cannot be recovered and must be written off.

Balance sheet Statement showing the assets and liabilities of a business at any particular moment.

Bankruptcy Where an individual or a business is unable to pay creditors in full. Being in a state of insolvency.

Base Rate UK interest rate set by the Bank of England Monetary Policy Committee for banks, etc. to follow.

Benchmark A set of standards or point of reference used in future measurements.

Benchmarking Looking at the way a successful business handles particular operational issues and comparing the performance of other businesses which face similar operational issues (not necessarily in the same industry) against that standard.

Benefits The advantages that a product or service will bring to the purchaser. Benefits are often derived from specific features of the product.

BFA British Franchising Association.

Bill of exchange A promise of payment (on a due date or on demand). It can be used as a means of obtaining payment from the buyer or it can be used as a method of obtaining trade finance.

Bill of lading Receipt for goods received aboard a vessel for transit. A transferable document of title to the goods.

Book value Value of an asset as shown in the accounting records.

Book-keeping Recording the financial transactions of a business in its books and keeping those accounts in order for review or VAT inspection.

Books The financial records of a business.

Brands Proprietary names (or trade mark names) which are used to identify the merchandise of particular manufacturers.

Break-even point Point at which income from sales exactly equals all the business costs.

British standards Standard definitions or specifications for the measurement, performance, safety, etc., of goods and/or services that are recognised in the UK.

Broker An agent who acts as a middleman in buying and selling (usually specialising, e.g. in insurance).

Budget Plan for the allocation and use of resources, often involving production of an itemised list of expected income and expenditure for a given period.

Business angel A private individual willing to invest in shares in a business.

Business Connect Welsh equivalent of Business Links.

Business Links Locally based centres in England which provide a point of reference for businesses seeking advice, access to information, Dti services, etc.

Business Names Act 1985 This Act covers the formulation and use of business names, and disclosure of ownership.

Business plan Detailed plan of future business activity.

Business rate *See* Uniform Business Rate.

Business Shops Scottish equivalent of Business Links.

Capital Finance invested by the proprietors in their business.

Capital Clause Clause within the Memorandum of Association stating the amount of authorised share capital and the amount and number of shares.

Capital Employed The net worth of the business (capital introduced plus retained profits) plus long-term loans. (Some definitions miss out long-term loans, others add short-term loans.)

Carnets An ATA Carnet is an international customs document issued by Chambers of Commerce which allow temporary importation of goods free of customs duties and taxes.

Cartel An informal arrangement between competing suppliers which acts to keep prices at an artificially high level. In most cases the practice is illegal. *See also* Restrictive Trade Practices.

Cash book This records all receipts and payments.

Cash flow The money coming into and going out of a business in a given period.

Cash flow forecast Projection of future cash flow.

CBI *see* Confederation of British Industry.

CE Mark A mark applied to a product to show that it complies with the 'essential requirements' of the EU Directives that cover that product. Certain types of product must carry a CE mark to be legally traded within the EU.

Certificate of Incorporation Issued by the Registrar of Companies when the incorporation of a company is authorised. It contains company name, number and date of incorporation. A company cannot lawfully trade without a valid Certificate.

Chamber of Commerce An association aimed at promoting trade.

CIMA The Chartered Institute of Management Accountants.

Collateral Security for a loan.

Companies House The more common name for the Registrar of Companies.

Company secretary By law, a company must have a company secretary. Their role is to ensure compliance with the secretarial requirements of the Companies Act.

Competitive advantage Something about a firm's product or service which gives it an edge over what competitors offer.

Components Stock items to be used in the manufacturing process.

Compulsory liquidation When a court orders the winding up of a company which has been unable to pay its creditors due to insolvency.

Conciliation The process of bringing two parties with different viewpoints into a position which suits both.

Confederation of British Industry Organisation representing the interests of British businesses.

Consolidated accounts The accounts of a parent/holding company which combine the accounts of subsidiary companies.

Constructive dismissal Also known as justified resignation. This is where an employer breaches the terms of the contract of employment and the employee resigns because of that breach.

Consultant A person from outside the business whose expertise is bought in when required.

Consumer Protection Act Legislation aimed at preserving the rights of consumers.

Contingency planning The process of identifying possible problems in the future and preparing plans of how these problems would be addressed.

Contingent liability A liability which is dependent upon future events.

Contract A legally binding agreement between two or more parties.

Control of Substances Hazardous to Health Regulations with which all businesses must comply for health and safety reasons.

Co-operatives Business owned and run by its members with all profits shared between the members.

Copyright A form of intellectual property – the automatic legal right of the originator of a piece of work to control the way in which their work is copied.

Corporate hospitality A way of maintaining contact with customers by inviting them to attend a special function.

Corporate planning Strategic planning across all parts of a business.

Corporate strategy The process of thinking about where the business is going, how the business relates to its market and how the business environment is changing.

Corporation Another word for company.

Corporation Tax Taxation on trading profits due to be paid by a company.

COSHH *See* Control of Substances Hazardous to Health.

Cost of sales Costs clearly attributable to production or provision of goods or services.

Costing Identifying the costs associated with business activities and sharing them out on a proportional basis.

Counselling The process of helping an individual to overcome problems by listening to what they have to say and prompting them with relevant questions.

County Court Local courts which handle civil cases involving claims for relatively low sums of money. Also known as the Small Claims Court.

Credit in A credit balance in your accounts reflects a liability because you owe money to your creditor.

Credit limit A limit on borrowing from a bank or supplier, or that you impose on your own customers.

Credit note Document given to a customer or given to you by a supplier to adjust for invoicing errors or return of faulty goods which shows that they are in credit to a certain amount.

Credit period Time allowed between the provision of goods or services and when they have to be paid for.

Credit referencing The process of checking on the credit-worthiness of someone. A number of agencies offer credit referencing services.

Creditors Those to whom money is owed for goods, cash, services, etc. Suppliers who are owed money are described as 'trade creditors' to differentiate them from others.

Creditors' voluntary winding up When a member's voluntary winding up resolution has been passed but the company proves to be insolvent it becomes a creditors' voluntary winding up.

Critical path analysis A project planning method which shows the relationships between tasks and the sequences in which they must be performed.

Current assets Assets in a cash or near cash state usually including debtors and stock.

Current liabilities Debts owed by a firm which have to be paid back within the next financial year.

Current ratio A financial ratio which measures the ratio of current assets to current liabilities.

Customer profiling An element of marketing. By a study of customers and their requirements, a profile of typical customers is drawn up.

Customs and Excise More correctly referred to as HM Customs and Excise. Government agency which controls imports and exports and collects customs duty, excise duty and VAT.

Data Protection Act Legislation that covers the storage and security of personal information held on computer databases.

Database A collection of information files.

Debenture loan A loan usually secured upon business assets.

Debit A record in the accounts of a sum owed to you.

Debt Money borrowed to finance the business.

Debtors Businesses or individuals who owe the business money.

Debtors' turnover ratio A measure of how quickly a firm's debtors pay their debts.

Depreciation A deduction from the book value of fixed assets over time.

Design right An intellectual property right. Designs for the configuration or shape of manufactured articles have automatic protection from copying in the UK. Novel designs can be given further protection if they are registered with the Patent Office.

Differentiation Where a firm designs its products or services specifically for particular customer types or market segments. *See also* Product differentiation.

Direct competition Where the product or service that one firm provides is essentially the same as that offered by another firm.

Direct costs Sometimes known as cost of sales, the costs that can be directly attributed to the production of a particular product or service.

Direct labour Workers directly involved in the production of goods and services.

Direct mail Selling products by mailing special sales literature directly to a selected list of potential customers.

Director An officer of the company responsible for compliance with the Companies Act and ensuring proper conduct in the daily operations of the company.

Directors' Duties Under the law, directors have a duty of care, and owe fiduciary duties to the company as a whole rather than to individual shareholders. Directors must also have regard to the interests of the employees as a whole.

Directors' Liabilities Directors may be held personally liable for irregularities in the way a company has operated. Offences may come to light during an audit or when an insolvent company goes into receivership or liquidation.

Disbursement Money paid out, especially as cash, for incidental expenses.

Disciplinary procedure The written procedure which a firm has said that it will follow in every case where an employee has to be reprimanded or ultimately dismissed.

Discount A deduction from the price of an item, or a bonus for prompt payment.

Discounted cash flow Technique for comparing projects to see which may give the better return on investment.

Distraint Seizure of a tenant's goods by a landlord for non-payment of debt.

Distribution The process of arranging for goods to be transferred from the point of production to the point of consumption.

Distributor Someone who is given the right to buy and sell a particular firm's products in a certain area or market.

Dividend The proportion of the company's profit after tax that will be paid to shareholders.

Double entry Method of book-keeping where every transaction is entered as a debit to one account and a credit to another account.

Drawings The money withdrawn by self-employed persons from their business.

Dti Department of Trade and Industry; the Government department responsible for business matters, including commercial and industrial development.

Duty A Government tax, most notably on imported goods.

Duty of care The responsibility to look after the welfare of others.

EFTPOS Electronic Funds Transfer at Point of Sale. Where equipment is used that debits the customer's bank or credit card account and credits the supplier's account automatically.

Embargo The official suspension of an activity such as trade. A press release is said to be embargoed if it is issued with a request to delay publication until after a specific date.

Employers' liability Employers may be held liable to pay compensation to employees who sustain personal injury or disease in the course of their employment or arising out of it. By law, all employers must take out insurance against such claims.

Enterprise agency An organisation which helps people to start up or expand a business. Services offered include: advice, training, managed workspace, loan funding and consultancy.

Entrepreneur Someone who takes initiatives in business as a manager. The term is often applied specifically to people who set up and run their own businesses.

Environment In business terms, the conditions in which a firm is operating.

Equity This is the capital introduced by the owners (shareholders), together with any retained earnings.

Euro The name of the single currency of the European Union.

Exchange rate The amount of foreign currency you will receive per £1 sterling.

Expenses General term which can mean all the costs of a business, but normally used to signify overhead expenses (as opposed to direct costs).

Export agent or distributor A representative covering the territory to which you are exporting, who may have exclusive rights to your product.

Export Credit Guarantee Department A department of the Dti providing export finance and insurance to exporters. *See also* NCM.

Export finance house A provider of medium- to long-term export credit.

Export licence A permit to export certain categories of goods covered by export controls, e.g. firearms, some computer parts, antiques and skins of endangered species.

Export Licensing Unit Advises exporters on whether or not they need a licence to export their goods.

Exporting Selling goods or services to other countries.

Extraordinary General Meeting (EGM) A meeting called by the directors of a company so that shareholders can consider proposed action which requires shareholder approval.

Extraordinary resolution This type of resolution must be passed by 75% of the shareholders attending and voting at the meeting. It is used for winding up an insolvent company.

Factor A provider of services, such as finance, on a manufacturer's behalf.

Factoring Handing a firm's debtor book to a third party agent who pays the firm a proportion of each debt when it falls due and any remainder, less a service charge, upon successful collection of the debt.

Features and Benefits In sales, the characteristics of a particular product. The features often translate into benefits which will appeal to the customer.

Fiduciary duties A director's duty to exercise his power as a director for the benefit of the company as a whole, and not to put themselves in a position where their duty to the company and their personal interests may conflict.

Financial ratio *See* Ratio Analysis

Financial year The 12-month period which a company chooses for its accounting year.

Fire Certificate A certificate confirming that premises have been inspected by the Fire Authority and that they meet relevant standards as required by law.

Firefighting Where managers are involved in dealing with one business crisis after another and are never in a position to step back and look at the overall position and direction of the firm.

Fixed assets Assets with a life of longer than one year, e.g. buildings, machinery, motor vehicles.

Fixed costs Costs which are fixed for the business for a reasonable length of time, and not dependent on the number of units produced, e.g. rent, rates, salaries.

Forecasting Predicting future situations, usually by identifying trends and taking past events into account.

Forward contract or forward foreign exchange contract A contract with a bank in which you agree to exchange a fixed amount of foreign currency on a fixed future date.

Franchising Where a business grants others a licence to produce, market or distribute products or services for which that business is known. The licence often allows the use of a trade name.

Fraudulent trading Carrying on company business with intent to commit fraud (e.g. by defrauding creditors). Anyone who knowingly trades fraudulently, or allows such trade to be carried out, may be personally liable to legal action.

Gearing A measure of debt as a proportion of total finance. The ratio of debt to equity.

Goodwill An intangible asset of a business, made up of regular customers, reputation, etc.

Usually taken into account if the business is sold.

Grants Financial assistance given to a business by a third party (e.g. a local authority). Grants do not usually have to be repaid provided agreed terms are met.

Grievance procedure A written set of steps which employees are required to follow if they wish to raise issues of concern with their employer.

Gross profit Normally the sales income less the direct costs.

Hire purchase Purchase method where the buyer pays a deposit then regular payments to cover cost plus interest.

Human resources The staff of an organisation.

ICAEW The Institute of Chartered Accountants in England and Wales.

IIP *See* Investors in People.

Import licence A licence required to import goods, usually needed when the allocation of foreign exchange is controlled.

Importing The process of buying things in from overseas.

Indirect costs Business costs that cannot be directly attributed to production of a particular product or service.

Industrial Common Ownership Movement (ICOM) Body that assists people to start and run businesses which are structured as co-operatives.

Input Tax VAT that a taxable business pays on the stock, materials and capital goods that it buys, and on goods or services it uses.

Insolvency The state of a business when it has insufficient assets to cover its liabilities as and when they fall due.

Intangible assets Items, such as goodwill, included as assets on the balance sheet because they have a perceived value but which have no physical form.

Intellectual property The ownership of ideas as developed in copyright, trade marks and patents.

Interest Money paid to a lender in return for use of their loan finance.

Interest cover Calculated as profit before interest and tax divided by interest paid.

Internet The name given to the network which connects computer systems all over the world.

Investors in People (IIP) A scheme which accredits businesses and other employers meeting a standard for staff development and training.

Invoice A document demanding payment for goods supplied.

Invoice discounting Where a third party pays an advance on the value of an invoice which is not yet due for payment.

ISO 9000 International standard for quality assurance procedures; incorporates the old British Standard BS5750. ISO is the International Standards Organisation.

Job description A statement given to an employee which outlines in general terms the purpose, scope and requirements of their post.

Joint and several liability The duty of directors to be liable both together and individually for the consequences of a breach of duty by the directors.

Journal In book-keeping, this is a book in which transactions are recorded with a note of which account each transaction will be debited and credited to.

Just-in-time A production system in which a manufacturer receives the exact number of supplies it requires at the point of production just before they are needed.

Key man Someone whose knowledge and/or skills are very important to the viability of a business.

Labelling The display of information about a product on its packaging. For various types of product (e.g. processed food, refrigeration equipment, etc.) the information given on the labels is required by law.

Lead time Time which must be allowed for something to happen (e.g. time between placing an order and its delivery).

Lease purchase A variation on leasing. At the end of the lease period the goods become the lessee's property.

Leasing Where the owner of property (e.g. premises, machinery) makes its use over to a business or individual for a specified period at an agreed rent.

Legislation Laws and the process of making them.

Lessee The party holding property on a lease from the owner.

Lessor The party owning property which is on lease to a lessee.

Letters of credit Agreement by which a buyer arranges with their bank for the seller to be paid, provided the seller can demonstrate that they have shipped the goods and obtained all the documents required by the letter of credit.

Liabilities Combined debts owed by a firm.

Liability A debt owed to someone else.

Limited company A company where the owners have limited liability. Companies can be public or private, and limited by shares or guarantee.

Limited partnership Partnership where one or more persons (general partners) are liable for all of the debts of the firm while one or more others (limited partners) contribute to the assets of the business by providing money or property but have no further liability for the firm's debts.

Liquid assets Cash or items that can readily be sold to convert into cash.

Liquidation Formal closing down of a business. Any assets are sold and used to pay off some or all of the firm's debts. Also known as winding up.

Liquidator A person or persons appointed to wind up a company by using assets to pay off liabilities.

Liquidity Measure of the working capital or cash available to a business to enable it to meet its liabilities as they fall due. Liquidity ratios include the current ratio and the quick ratio.

Loans Funds borrowed by a business, repaid over an agreed period with interest.

Loss Where expenditure exceeds income in a given period.

Loss leader Product sold at a loss to attract customers for other products.

Management accounts Detailed financial information provided with the needs of business managers in mind.

Management buy-in Where a new owner buys an existing business and takes on a management role.

Management buy-out Where the managers of a company, or a division of a larger company buy it from its owners and run it as an independent business in its own right.

Management consultancy A service where a consultant is paid to advise the people in control of a business on the systems and procedures that they could or should adopt.

Marginal cost The extra cost incurred by producing one extra unit.

Market Customers or potential customers that can be identified by common characteristics such as location or buying requirements.

Market research Research to provide management with data about current or potential customers, competitors, trends, etc. which can be used in decision making.

Market segmentation The process of defining the prominent characteristics of a firm's customers. Most markets can be divided up into distinct sections based on criteria such as customer location, age, industry sector.

Marketing Planning to provide customers with the goods and/or services that they want and to make a profit in the process.

Marketing mix The marketing strategy, covering decisions concerning the product or service, position within the market, price, and methods of promotion.

Market-led An approach to running a business where the customers' needs are identified and then the product or service is developed to meet those needs.

Mark-up Difference in the price of goods or services introduced by a supplier. A manufacturer might add a mark-up to the cost of manufacturing to provide a profit. A retailer might add a further mark-up to cover overheads and generate profit.

Members The shareholders of a company.

Members' voluntary winding up The winding up of a solvent business by a resolution of the shareholders.

Memorandum of association The memorandum covers the company's external relations. It consists of six clauses: name clause; domicile clause; objects clause; capital clause; limitation of liability clause and the association clause.

Mentoring The provision of support and guidance to someone by assigning another (usually more experienced or senior) person to take responsibility for providing that support and guidance.

Mezzanine finance An arrangement giving a business additional funding, made up of both equity capital and debt.

Minutes Records of what was said and agreed at official meetings. Once written up, minutes are accepted as a true representation of the proceedings by those present (usually at the next meeting) and may be signed off.

Misrepresentation Giving a false or misleading impression about something.

Mission statement A statement outlining the purpose of the business; it may also include a description of the vision.

Monopoly Where one supplier controls at least a third of the market for particular goods or services.

MOPS Mail Order Protection Scheme; a scheme operated by various publishers who take advertising from firms who sell by mail order. The scheme is designed to give consumers who respond to the advertising a degree of protection.

National Insurance (NI) Government-operated scheme of insurance against ill health and unemployment. Partly funds the NHS, unemployment benefits, state pensions, etc. Both employers and employees contribute to the scheme.

NCM (Nederlandsche Credietverzekering Maatschappij N. V.) A credit insurer who took over the running of part of the Export Credit Guarantee Department (ECGD) in 1991.

Negative cash flow Where more money is going out of the business than is coming in.

Negotiation The process of trying to reach agreement through discussion.

Net current assets Current assets minus current liabilities. This should be positive, otherwise the business may not be able to meet debts as they fall due.

Net profit The amount remaining after all costs of running the business have been deducted from the income.

Net profit margin Net profit divided by sales and expressed as a percentage.

Net worth Total assets less total liabilities.

Networking Building up and exploiting a network of useful business contacts.

Non-executive director A director who is not directly involved with the day-to-day management of a company. Usually appointed to bring advice and experience.

Not-for-profit organisation Usually refers to charities, voluntary sector organisations and other bodies set up to meet a social need. Any excess of income over expenditure is retained within the organisation for future use. Such organisations may take the legal form of a company limited by guarantee.

Office of National Statistics (ONS) Government agency responsible for the collation and publication of statistics on economic and social matters.

Official Receiver A receiver who is an officer of the DTI, appointed by the High Court to oversee the liquidation of a business during a compulsory winding up (compulsory liquidation).

Ombudsman Official responsible for investigating complaints and disputes in a particular field such as banking, pensions or insurance.

Open account A payment term which means that the buyer only pays after receipt of the goods, usually on a monthly basis.

Operating profit Actual profit made by the business after deduction of all expenses except interest.

Opportunity cost Lost income or profit which would have been earned if a different choice had been made. Any investment choice can be compared with other options in advance to predict which will earn, or in retrospect to see which would have earned, the most.

Ordinary resolution This type of resolution needs only a majority of shareholders to attend a meeting and pass the resolution.

Ordinary Share A share in the company that is not repayable. The shareholder's investment can only be recovered by selling the share. On the winding up of the company ordinary shareholders are a low priority for repayment.

Output Tax VAT due on taxable goods or services supplied to a customer.

Out-sourcing Buying in goods or services rather than producing them in-house.

Overdraft Funding provided by a bank allowing money to be withdrawn from a current account. An overdraft limit (the maximum amount they will allow the customer to go overdrawn by) will be agreed and interest will be charged on the amount borrowed.

Overhead costs All operating costs which are not direct and which, generally speaking, are fixed costs.

Overtrading When a business is selling more products or services than the working capital facilities can cope with.

Own brand Where a firm sells products under its own name rather than that of the manufacturer.

Pareto Analysis using the 20/80 rule to identify the areas which merit most management attention. The rule assumes that 20% of customers represent 80% of sales.

Partnership A business that is owned by more than one individual but which is not a limited company. See also Limited partnership.

Patent agent Professional whose job is to research and apply for patents on behalf of clients.

Patents A form of intellectual property. Granted to the inventors of items or processes. A patent confers the sole right to make, use or sell the invention. UK patents are registered with the Patent Office which can advise on all intellectual property matters.

PAYE (Pay As You Earn) All employers are required to deduct income tax from employees' pay. The system uses tax codes to adjust the level of deductions from each employee's pay.

Payment terms The terms which the customer is required to meet when making payment under a contract.

Payroll The list of a firm's employees who receive regular payments.

Performance appraisal The process of evaluating an employee's performance, usually against previously agreed targets and the requirements of their post as outlined in their job description.

Performance related pay Pay which is directly linked to achievement against agreed targets.

Personnel The employees of an organisation.

Personnel management The discipline of managing personnel to get the best out of them.

PESTE analysis A method of assessing the environment and its impact on the business – through examining political, economic, social, technological and environmental trends and influences.

Picketing Where a group of workers with a grievance against an employer post themselves at the entrance to the employer's premises to demonstrate their feelings and deter other workers from going into work. May be used in conjunction with strike action.

Piece work Employment where the worker is paid at an agreed rate for each item that they produce.

Place In the marketing mix, the location of the market and the means of distribution used to get products or services to that market.

Plant A factory and its machinery.

Point-of-Sale (POS) Place where the sales transaction takes place. Usually used in a retail context. The promotion of consumer goods may use point-of-sale display materials.

Policy statement A document outlining the way in which a business intends to act in certain circumstances.

Positive cash flow Where more money is coming into the business than is going out of it.

Preference share A type of share in a company. A preference shareholder may receive a larger dividend that an ordinary shareholder. They also have higher priority for repayment if a company is wound up.

Preferential debts Debts, for example taxes, which must be paid first when a company goes into liquidation.

Prepayments Payments made in advance where the benefit has not yet been received.

Price In the marketing mix, the setting of the price to be charged, usually at what the market will bear, to maximise the profit to the business.

Pro forma invoice An invoice sent in advance of the supply of goods.

Product In the marketing mix, the development of the product or service which most closely meets the requirements of a specific market whilst retaining or increasing market share and profitability.

Product differentiation Using the unique feature (or combination of features) that your product possesses, and your competitors' products do not,

to interest prospective customers.

Profit Level by which income exceeds expenditure in a given period.

Profit and loss account Summary of all income and expenditure for a defined accounting period.

Profit margin Ratio of profit to sales calculated using either gross profit or net profit and expressed as a percentage.

Project management Using recognised methods to plan and manage the various stages of a project.

Promotion In the marketing mix, the choice of methods for bringing the product to the attention of potential customers and motivating them to buy it.

Proxy A person who acts on the behalf of a shareholder. They will normally attend the Annual General Meeting or Extraordinary General Meeting and vote as directed by the shareholder.

Public Limited Company (plc) A limited company whose Memorandum of Association states that it is a public company. The company must have a minimum allotted capital of £50,000.

Public Relations (PR) Planned activity to give the public a positive impression of the business.

Purchase ledger Used to record all suppliers' invoices and payments to suppliers, and to show which are unpaid.

Purchasing The process of buying in supplies, includes negotiation, ordering and chasing delivery.

Pyramid selling A form of selling, illegal in the UK, where someone buys the rights to sell a product; to succeed they must then sell other people the right to sell the product. Sales of the product become secondary to selling the right to sell the product.

Qualified accounts Audited company accounts where the auditor has expressed doubts or disagreement over the information shown in the accounts.

Questionnaire A list of questions to be asked. Used in a survey to ensure that everyone is answering the same questions so that answers can be compared and analysed.

Quick ratio A financial ratio which measures how readily a firm can pay off its debts. It is the ratio of cash and debtors to current liabilities. Also called acid test ratio.

Quorum A quorum is the number of shareholders required to be present, either in person or by proxy, at the beginning of a general meeting, before business can be transacted.

Quotation An offer to provide specific goods or services at a specified price.

R & D *See* Research and Development.

Racial equality The principle that everyone is equal regardless of their ethnic origin.

Ratio analysis Reviewing a firm's performance by looking at the way particular figures in the accounts relate to each other.

Raw materials The most basic ingredients used in a production process.

Receiver A person who takes control of property which has been charged with debt. They will only take control of the property to which the debt is charged and nothing else. They have less power than an administrative receiver.

Receivership Where a bankrupt firm's affairs are being administered by a court-appointed receiver.

Recourse In a credit transaction, if a buyer fails to pay in accordance with the agreement then the bank (or other party) which has paid and failed to recover the payments can claim the payments from the exporter.

Recruitment The process of finding new staff. May involve advertising, reviewing applications and interviewing a short-list of suitable candidates.

Reducing balance Method of accounting for the depreciation of a fixed asset over its expected useful life.

Redundancy Where there is no longer a need for someone to carry out a particular function within an organisation, anyone employed specifically to perform that function is redundant. If staff are dismissed due to redundancy they may be entitled to compensation.

Regional Selective Assistance (RSA) Government funding which is intended to promote economic regeneration within defined geographical areas. Usually in the form of grant aid to businesses setting up a new operation in, or relocating to, that area.

Registered number The unique number by which a company is recorded at Companies House.

Registered office An official address for a company at which documents can be served. Many companies use their solicitor or accountant's office.

Registrar of Companies Often referred to as Companies House, it holds public documents for all registered companies, listed and unlisted, past and present.

Relocation Moving a business or members of staff from one site to another.

RemunerationThe financial rewards of employment, including salary, bonuses, pension schemes, company cars, etc.

Research and development The process of coming up with new products or processes, often through technical or scientific innovation. May result in the ownership of intellectual property.

Reserves Profits retained within the business.

Resolution Shareholders make decisions at the Annual General Meeting or Extraordinary General Meeting by passing resolutions. There are four types of resolution: ordinary, extraordinary, elective, and special.

Restraint of trade Where clauses in a contract of employment seek to prevent an employee who leaves from exploiting knowledge gained whilst with the employer. Such clauses are illegal unless the employer can show that they are needed to protect the business.

Restrictive trade practices Trading practices or agreements which are not in the public interest. These may include the operation of a cartel or the unfair exploitation of a monopoly.

Retail Selling direct to the consumer via a shop or similar outlet.

Retail Prices Index An official measure of the change over time of the value of money.

Return on investment Amount of money generated in a given period of time for the investment of a given amount of capital.

Revenue Income generated by the business for a specific period.

Revenue account Record of company income and expenditure which excludes capital income and expenditure.

Revolving credit A letter of credit that is designed to cover continuing trade over a period of time. It allows the reinstatement of the amount available for drawings in accordance with specified criteria.

Risk assessment The basic principle of all recent health and safety legislation is that anyone with a legal duty to provide a safe working environment should carry out a thorough assessment of all of the risks that might be encountered.

Risk management The process of analysing and evaluating the potential risks associated with a course of action and devising ways of removing or minimising the risks and reducing their harmful effects.

Salary Regular payments to an employee, usually on a monthly basis.

Sales ledger Record of every invoice issued, the amount of cash received and the amount due to the business.

Sales promotion Activities other than direct selling, such as competitions, advertising, public relations, samples, etc. which promote sales of a product or service.

Sampling Statistical approach to a survey where data is collected from a group which represents the population being studied rather than trying to collect data from everyone in that population.

Scenario planning The process of establishing what future environmental circumstances are possible, and identifying how the company would respond to these different circumstances.

Security A guarantee given by a borrower to a lender to safeguard a loan. The lender may be given a prior charge over assets.

Self assessment The Government has now made many individuals responsible for calculating their own tax liability and reporting the details to the Inland Revenue.

Self-employed Where someone is working or in business on their own behalf rather than for an employer. The business can employ others but cannot be a limited company.

Share capital Capital raised by issuing shares.

Shareholders Owners of a company's shares or stocks.

Shares The ownership of a company is divided into shares, each representing a part of the equity capital invested in the business.

Shelf company A ready-made company that can be bought from solicitors and other professional advisors. Commonly costing between £100 and £400, these can be the quickest way of getting a limited company up and running.

Shrinkage Loss of stock through deterioration, waste or theft.

Small Claims Court The County Court. Small claims are claims of up to £5,000 for reasons such as breach of contract, failure to pay and personal injury.

Small Company Audit Exemption Regulations Regulations providing exemption from statutory audit requirements for private companies with turnovers below defined levels.

SME Small to Medium-sized Enterprise.

Soft loan Loan made at a low interest rate. Some loans are called soft loans because they have lenient repayment terms.

Software The programs and data that a computer uses to operate.

Sole trader Someone who is carrying on a business in their own name.

Solvency Measure of a business's ability to pay its bills as they fall due. If it cannot pay, then it is insolvent. A negative net worth indicates a business is insolvent.

Special resolution This type of resolution requires 21 days notice of hearing and must be passed by 75% of the shareholders present and voting at the meeting.

Spot rate An exchange rate quoted on the spot date. It reflects the relative strengths of the economies and the respective buying power of the currencies at that date.

Spreadsheet A computer software program displaying rows and columns of numbers (and text). They are useful for cash flow analysis, producing budgets, etc.

Staged payments Payment by instalments.

Standard Industrial Classification (SIC) A SIC code is a numerical representation of the principal industry in which a business operates. Used by Government and other organisations to divide up business data by activity.

Start-up costs Costs specifically associated with setting up in business.

Statutory books Also referred to as company books. They consist of registers of information, three of which are required by law: directors and secretaries; directors' interests; and shareholders.

Statutory duties Directors' duties imposed by the Government. They cover areas such as: exercising appropriate care and skill; keeping proper accounting records and statutory books; disclosure of personal interest in contracts; filing required documents with Companies House; and observing restrictions on loans from the company and the transfer of company assets.

Statutory sick pay Scheme whereby employees who were absent from work due to medical incapacity receive a guaranteed minimum income if they meet certain conditions.

Stock Goods held for sale in the ordinary course of business. Raw materials, components and consumables may also be held in stock.

Stock control Active management of the level of holding of raw materials, components, and finished goods to ensure that money is not tied up unnecessarily.

Stock Exchange A centre where shares in public companies are traded.

Straight line Method of accounting for the depreciation of a fixed asset across its estimated useful life.

Strategic objectives The objectives that have been identified as necessary if the vision is to be realised.

Strategic planning Planning of the overall direction of the business.

Strike The withdrawal of labour by employees, usually due to an unresolved dispute.

Subcontracting Where a contract holder makes contracts with other firms to supply goods or services required as part of the main contract.

Subscribers Two or more people who together set up a company. They sign the association clause in the Memorandum of Association and agree the Articles of Association, becoming shareholders.

Subsidiary company A business which is controlled by another company.

Supplier A provider of goods or services.

SWOT analysis A technique for summarising the strengths, weaknesses, opportunities and threats of a business.

Table A The Articles of Association provided by Government regulations for companies that do not provide their own.

Take-over Where one business gains control of another, either by buying up a controlling interest in the equity of the firm or by a direct cash payment.

Tangible assets Real assets which belong to a firm, and are not intended for resale; e.g. premises, machinery, etc., but not stock or goodwill.

Target market A specific market sector identified through market segmentation which the business has decided to concentrate upon selling into.

Taxable supplies Goods and services supplied to a customer which are liable for VAT.

Taxable turnover Total value of taxable supplies including VAT. Excludes any exempt goods and services.

Telemarketing Conducting research, sales and marketing activities over the telephone.

Telesales Selling over the telephone.

Teleworking Working from a remote location using telecommunications to make up for the absence of direct contact.

Temporary employees (Temps) Staff who are on short-term contracts or who are hired through an agency to fill in at periods of high demand or when permanent staff are temporarily absent.

Test marketing A market research technique involving the marketing of the product or service on a small scale before expanding production or availability.

Total quality management Running an organisation with a systematic approach to customer satisfaction through continuous improvement throughout the organisation.

Trade association An association whose members are businesses with common concerns, often being in the same industry.

Trade mission A co-ordinated overseas visit designed to help a number of businesses to meet potential buyers and/or agents. Often arranged by Chambers of Commerce.

Trade union An organisation whose members are employees, often related by type of employer or trade. They represent employee interests in negotiations with employers.

Trademarks A form of intellectual property. Trade marks are logos or wording which manufacturers use to make their products readily identifiable. They can be registered to prevent other firms from copying them.

Trading Standards A local authority department responsible for enforcing elements of consumer protection legislation.

Training Organised activity aimed at adding to or enhancing the skills and expertise of personnel.

Transfer of undertakings Where the ownership of, or controlling interest in, a business or other similar organisation changes from one person, or group of people, to another.

Trial balance In double entry book-keeping, checking to see if all debit and credit items in a ledger have the same total.

Turnkey system A self-contained system, ready to run upon delivery without modification.

Turnover Total sales income. Net turnover is total sales less returns (excluding VAT).

Uniform Customs and Practice for Documentary Credits A set of rules that covers the operation of letters of credit. These rules have been devised by the ICC but are not enforceable by law unless stipulated in the letter of credit.

Ultra vires An action by a company or director which goes beyond the activities allowed in the objects clause of the Memorandum of Association.

Unfair dismissal Dismissal of an employee from their post in a manner which is considered as unfair by an industrial tribunal.

Uniform Business Rate The amount by which the rateable value of non-domestic premises is multiplied to arrive at the amount payable in a given year.

Unique Selling Point (USP) The positive feature which makes a product or service stand out from its competitors.

Value Added Tax (VAT) Taxation on consumer spending which applies to the value added to a product at each stage of its production and distribution. VAT is collected in stages by VAT registered firms.

Value chain analysis Looking at every stage of the process of supplying goods or services to identify at which stages value is added and where there is room to trim out elements which incur unnecessary or excessive cost.

Variable costs Costs which vary with production levels, e.g. direct costs such as raw materials. However, other costs, such as power consumption, may also vary and these need to be taken into account.

Venture capital Funding which may be made available to businesses with good prospects of growth. Venture capital providers often take a significant involvement in the business.

Virtual office Home-based workers using teleworking to work in a group and carry out the same functions as if they were based in an office.

Vision Where the business is going, a statement of desired competitive position outlining challenging but achievable goals with defined time-scales.

Voluntary arrangement An agreement between an insolvent company and its creditors, which allows the company to continue to trade whilst it pays off its debts over an agreed time-scale. This may avoid liquidation.

Voluntary redundancy Where an employee chooses to accept redundancy when the employer is restructuring its staffing levels. Employees are usually offered favourable terms for volunteering.

Wages Regular payments to an employee, usually on a weekly basis.

Wages book Records wages and salary payments made to employees.

Warranty A guarantee, usually part of a contract for the supply of goods or services.

Website An distinct area of the World Wide Web where information on a particular topic can be found. A site is made up of web pages and is usually linked to other sites using Hypertext links.

Wholesale Where a middleman works between a supplier and a retailer, often providing local warehousing and breaking bulk consignments into smaller lots.

Winding up This is a method of dissolving a company and is also known as liquidation.

Work in Progress Raw materials, components and products which are within the production process but are not yet finished goods.

Working capital The difference between current assets and current liabilities.

World Wide Web A part of the Internet. The Web is made up of a vast number of inter-linked websites.

Write off To reduce the value of an asset in the books to zero, for example to record a debt as being a bad debt.

Written down value When the book value of an asset is reduced to take depreciation into account, the new value is the written down value.

Wrongful dismissal Dismissal of an employee in a manner which breaches their common law rights.

Wrongful trading Allowing the business to continue trading when insolvency is inevitable. Any director who knew, or ought to have known, that their company could not avoid becoming insolvent may be personally liable to make payments into company assets if they failed to take all possible steps to minimise creditors' losses.

Index